REAL LIFE GUIDE TO

Graduate and Professional School

How to Choose, Apply For, and Finance Your Advanced Degree!

REAL LIFE GUIDE TO

Graduate and Professional School

How to Choose, Apply For, and Finance Your Advanced Degree!

Cynthia L. Rold, J.D.

PIPELINE

ISBN 1-890586-05-6

Printed in the United States of America

"Real Life Guide"™ Pipeline Press, Inc.

Published by:
Pipeline Press, Inc.
PO Box 9255
Chapel Hill, NC 27515-9255
http://www.pipelinepress.com

Distributed by:
Associated Publishers Group
1501 County Hospital Rd.
Nashville, TN 37218
800-327-5113

10 9 8 7 6 5 4 3 2 1

Trademarks

Trademarked names appear throughout this book. Rather than list the names and entities that own the trademarks or insert a trademark symbol with each mention of the trademarked name, the publisher states that it is using the names only for editorial purposes and to the benefit of the trademark owner with no intention of infringing upon that trademark.

Credits

Managing Editor	Kerry L.B. Foster
Developmental Editor	Laura Poole
Copy Editor	Heather R. Valli
Layout	Anny B. Thompson
Cover Design	Mike Benson Design / Tina Clossick
Print Production	Paula Hershman
CD Production	R. Allen Wyke
Publisher	Joel Bush

Special Thanks

EMJ Inc., Associated Publishers Group, The Word Factory, BookMasters, beginners.com, Enter Magazine, Lassiter Presort, MindSpring Enterprises, ForeFront Group, Fotel, WinWay, Johanna Christensen, Jack Peterson, James January, and Eric Coker

About the Author

Cynthia L. Rold, JD, learned about the admissions process while working as the dean of admissions at Duke University School of Law and the University of Illinois College of Law. She had her own real-life introduction to the admissions process when she applied and was admitted to Northwestern University School of Law, where she obtained her law degree. She received her BA degree magna cum laude from Carroll College in Waukesha, Wisconsin. Ms. Rold has been involved in many aspects of law school administration, and she served a year as president of the National Association for Law Placement.

Contents

Section 2 How to Get the Ball Rolling

Section 3 Making It Happen

Section 4 Moving On

Introduction

If you have finished or are about to finish four years of college, you may be wondering what's next. You may know that a graduate or professional degree is required for the type of job you want. Or, after spending 16 years in school, you may be paralyzed at the thought of not going to school anymore. If that is true for you, your thoughts will naturally turn to graduate or professional school because it's the most logical way to continue being a student.

If you feel liberated at the thought of no more school, you may not be interested in thinking about graduate or professional school right now. It's possible that after working for a few years, you will decide you want to earn an additional degree because the job is not providing the level of intellectual stimulation or financial reward that you would like. You may also find that you miss being in an academic environment.

Penelope thought about getting a master's degree in social work right after she graduated from college, but she wasn't sure she was ready for more school at that point. She thought it was a good idea to work and get some experience first. She found a job working for a social services agency, and after three years, she found that she was ready to attend graduate school.

Who This Book Is For

If you think that graduate or professional school is somewhere in your future, either next year or within the next few years, this book is for you. It is full of information and inspiration that will help you get through the sometimes bewildering process of choosing the right program, applying, getting financial aid, and choosing the school you want to attend. Because schools begin accepting applications almost a year before you will start school, and you have to take a standardized test before you can apply, it is wise to start preparing early. You don't want to wait until May and then try to get into a school for the following August.

What This Book Will Offer You

There are a number of things you can do to increase your chances of being admitted, some of which require time and planning. Those techniques are covered in Chapter 6.

If you already know what type of degree you want to pursue, you will find sections in each chapter that cover the following degree programs: business, law, medicine, doctoral, and master's. You will be able to read the general information at the beginning of those chapters and the specific sections pertaining to your degree program. You will find yourself armed with valuable insights that will make the application process much smoother. Worksheets are included to help you organize your admissions and financial aid materials and to compare and contrast different schools.

If you are just beginning to think about attending graduate or professional school or you know for sure that you want to go, but you don't know what degree you want, this book will be quite helpful. By reading the entire book, you will have an excellent understanding of graduate degrees, both master's and doctoral, and of professional degrees, including business, law, and medicine. Chapter 2 will help you assess which program is right for you, and Chapter 10 will let you know what kind of career options are available to you with the different degrees.

All readers will find the Resources chapter to be extremely valuable, as it points you to other sources of information available both electronically and in print.

What This Book Will Not Do

The path that leads from the idea of graduate or professional school to graduation can be long, but you can make it less arduous by being well-informed. You have made a good decision to start by reading this book which will help you by giving you inspiration, motivation, and above all, good advice. Reading this book does not guarantee that you will get into graduate or professional school or that you will get a full scholarship. It is not a quick fix and requires that you do a lot of hard work. Good luck, and have a great time.

Section 1

Where to Start

chapter 1

Overview

Perhaps the farthest your grandfather got in his education was the twelfth grade. Upon graduation, he may have found a job he enjoyed and stayed with it until retirement, advancing the entire time he worked there. This was not uncommon in those days. When your parents went to school, they found that it was harder to get ahead with just a high school diploma. Even though they might have been hired with only a high school diploma, they probably hit a ceiling and couldn't advance beyond a certain point. So they found that it was important to get a college degree if they wanted to get to the same level your grandfather reached. Now many people feel that they have to have an advanced degree in order to get beyond a certain point in their careers. Perhaps you are feeling that way, which is one reason why you are reading this book.

Attending graduate or professional school is a big step and should not be taken lightly. You'll want to consider carefully whether an advanced degree will help you in the ways you think it will. This book can assist you in making that determination. You're probably wondering how you will select a school, how you will pay for it, and what you have to do to be admitted. Each of those issues will be addressed in this book.

There are many reasons for pursuing a graduate or professional degree, but not all of them are appropriate. One of the more common and least compelling reasons to pursue an advanced degree is that you aren't sure what else to do with your life. Before committing the time, money, and energy required to obtain an advanced degree, it is important to have a clear idea of why you want to get the degree and what you hope to do with it once you have obtained it. Chapter 2 will cover this topic in greater detail, but for now, we'll point out some of the more common reasons for obtaining an advanced degree. They include the following:

- It is required for the type of career you want to pursue (i.e., being a doctor, teaching at a university, or a host of other careers).
- It will provide you with a higher salary than you could obtain without it.
- You are interested in a particular field and want to study it in more depth.
- You want to advance in your current field, and you will be unable to do that without an advanced degree, no matter how talented you are.
- You want to change careers.
- You want an intellectual challenge and an interesting experience.
- The job market is bad, and perhaps it won't be as bad when you graduate with an advanced degree, or at least the advanced degree will make you more employable, even if the job market remains weak.

Graduate and professional school is not the right choice for everyone. It's important that you spend a lot of time thinking about whether it's right for you. We'll cover this topic in some depth in Chapter 2, but for now, some general questions to ask yourself are:

- Am I really interested in this field?
- Have I talked to a number of people who have gotten degrees in this field, and do I have a good sense of why they are happy or unhappy with their choices?
- Do I have the time, money, and energy needed to commit to this degree for the required amount of time?
- Have I considered the job market in my chosen field? Am I likely to be able to find the type of job I want with this degree?
- Have I contacted professional associations in my field to get information about graduate programs and career opportunities? (A list of associations is provided in Chapter 11.)

If you're not sure whether graduate or professional school is right for you, work for a year or two after college to get experience and determine what you want to do next.

Timing is an important consideration when considering graduate or professional school. A common question is whether it is better to attend graduate or professional school right after college or to wait for a few years. With respect to getting admitted into a graduate or professional school program, there is no clear answer as to whether one route is better than the other. This really is a personal decision that should be based on your preferences and goals rather than on how it will affect the admissions decision.

Working for one year or five years between college and graduate or professional school can be wonderful if you are not sure what you want to do. You can work in an industry that you think interests you and gain more insight into whether that field is really the one you want to pursue and what degree you need in order to pursue it. Working in the field you intend to enter can sometimes help you in the admissions process, although it depends on the type of program to which you are applying and the particular school to which you are applying.

Working in any field, regardless of whether it is related to the subject you eventually decide to study, can broaden your perspectives and allow you to see interrelationships between areas that you might not have noticed before. Working for a few years after college also allows you to mature and experience life outside of an academic institution, probably for the first time since you entered kindergarten. This can help you to keep your graduate schoolwork in perspective when you encounter some of the inevitable rough spots.

The list of possible jobs is endless. You've probably thought of the obvious examples for your particular field, like working in a hospital or for a doctor if you want to go to medical school, getting a research job in a related field if you're considering graduate school, working for a law firm if you're thinking about law school, or finding a corporate job if you'd like to get an MBA. But what about some nontraditional alternatives that you might not have thought about? Some of these suggestions may be more directly applicable to one particular field than another, but again, remember, this is the time for you to experiment and do something different. You don't have to get a job that will directly prepare you for graduate or professional school.

- The Peace Corps is a fascinating experience for many and lasts for two years, so it's a nice, defined period of time.
- Some applicants want to get their international experience in other ways and will find a job teaching English overseas.
- Working in politics is a popular choice, either on the Hill (Capitol Hill, that is), or in their state legislature.

If you have a secret passion you want to pursue, now may be the time. You could write that novel you've been dreaming about, work as a trapeze artist (yes, an applicant really did that and was admitted to law school), or be an entrepreneur and start your own company.

The point is that your choice of jobs is limited only by your imagination. All too often, recent graduates focus only on jobs that they think will help them get into graduate or professional school later. If your academic record is poor, then it may be helpful to work in the field you want to enter in order to show that you are capable of doing that kind of work. If your record is strong, then you don't need to worry about "padding your résumé" just for admission purposes.

However, if you know what type of degree you want to pursue and you are certain that you want to get it directly after college, there is no reason not to apply immediately.

The following chart gives you an idea of how long many people wait to get an advanced degree after getting their bachelor's degree. In education, it is quite common for people to work for a number of years before getting their PhD, while in the sciences and engineering, it is more common to begin your PhD immediately after graduating from college.

Median Number of Years Between BA and PhD	
Education	19.9
Business & Management	12.1
Arts & Humanities	12.0
Social Sciences	10.5
Life Sciences	9.5
Engineering	9.1
Physical Sciences	8.4
All Fields	10.9

What Is Graduate and Professional School?

Some people assume that all study beyond the undergraduate level is graduate school. However, there is a distinction between graduate and professional school. Professional school is post-undergraduate study that prepares you to enter a specific profession. Professional schools include law, business, medicine, and dentistry. Graduate school is advanced study in a department that offers an undergraduate degree in that field as well. In this book, graduate school encompasses all post-undergraduate study that is not professional school and will deal both with master's degrees and doctorates.

Typically, a professional school is a school within the university that has a great deal of autonomy and freedom from university regulations. It will usually have its own facilities, including its own building, and often its own registrar, career services office, and financial aid office. Sometimes a professional school will use a different calendar than the rest of the university and may use a different grading scale.

The graduate school may also be a school or college within the university; however, it exists to meet the needs of all graduate students, regardless of their discipline. Just as the university is the administrative body for most undergraduates, the graduate school is the administrative body for graduate students. While graduate students will have some dealings with the graduate school, most of their dealings will be with their own department in the field they are studying. This can sometimes create confusion for students, especially during the admissions process, so you should ask each university which office handles which matters.

Graduate and professional schools are very different from undergraduate school due to the nature of the study. Rather than learning about a number of unrelated subjects as you did in college, you become immersed in one area in depth. Although there is variety in that area, it is more comparable to taking classes in your major throughout your time in graduate or professional school. The teaching and learning methods are also very different in graduate and professional school.

Law schools use the Socratic method; business schools use the case method approach, coupled with small group interaction; medical schools require vast amounts of memorization and little faculty-student interaction for the first couple of years; and graduate school requires you to be a very independent, self-directed learner. The next sections will examine each of these programs in a little more depth. A detailed discussion of each of these programs is contained in Chapter 7.

Law School

Students attend law school for the equivalent of three years of full-time study before receiving a JD (Juris Doctorate) degree. The first year consists of required courses, while the next two years are made up almost entirely of elective courses. Students study cases, which are actual court opinions from previously decided cases. Students learn the law by analyzing and learning the underlying themes from the cases. The teaching method used in many classes, particularly in the first year, is the Socratic method. This involves the teacher engaging a student or students in a series of questions relating to the case that was read for that class.

Business School

An MBA program requires the equivalent of two years of full-time study to complete. Traditional lectures, where the professor lectures and you, the student, take notes, are still relatively common in business schools. A number of schools also use the case method, which involves reading a complex case involving a business situation (either real or fictional) and then analyzing the case and resolving a particular issue or issues. Another method of teaching is to use computer simulation, where students engage in team competitions using a simulated problem. They enter data into a computer about various alternatives they have chosen for the company they are "managing," and the computer determines which teams have made the best decisions.

Medical School

Students receive their medical degrees after attending the equivalent of four years of full-time study. The first year generally covers aspects of normal human biology and consists of large lectures for about half the time and labs for the other half. The second year focuses on abnormal human biology, and students continue to attend lectures and labs. They will also have clinical pathological conferences during this year. In the third year, the emphasis is on diagnosing disease, and students will have considerable exposure to clinical experience during this year. The last year is almost entirely clinical. After attending medical school and receiving the medical degree, a student must still complete a residency, which can take from one to ten years, depending on the specialty or subspecialty chosen.

Graduate School

In graduate school you may choose to earn either a master's degree or a doctoral degree. Although the programs have some similarities, they are quite different in length and, depending on the program, may also be quite different in focus. Due to their differences each is considered independently.

Master's Degree

Master's degree programs typically last for two years, although some may only require one year of study. You may earn a terminal master's degree, or you may be awarded a master's degree on the way to getting your PhD. Students are generally on either the academic track or the practical track. The academic track focuses on research and scholarship, and is typically the proving ground for the PhD. The practical track provides practical training that allows a graduate to enter or advance in a specialized field. If you are on the academic track, you will be required to write a thesis before you graduate. If you are on the practical track, your program may require fieldwork.

Doctoral Degree

In a PhD program you will complete basic coursework during the first year or two and then will take qualifying or field exams, which may be oral in nature. After you have passed those examinations that show you have a basic mastery of the subject, you will engage in independent, in-depth research into a particular area, culminating in a thesis. Under normal circumstances, it can take anywhere from four to seven years to receive your PhD. However, if you manage to complete all of the requirements for the PhD except for the thesis and you let the thesis drag on, it could take a very long time for you to get your PhD.

Number of Years Required for Degree	
Master's	1–2 years
Doctorate	4–7 years
MBA	2 years
Law	3 years
Medicine	4 years

The following table will give you an idea of which fields are the most popular for students pursuing doctoral degrees.

Number of Doctorates Granted by Field in 1995	
Education	6,546
Engineering	6,007
Psychology	3,267
Chemistry	2,161
Physics, Astronomy	1,652
Mathematics	1,190
Computer Science	998
Economics	954
History	889
Earth, Atmospheric, Marine Science	805
English	753
Music	713
Political Science	600
Sociology	539
Anthropology	375
Philosophy	298
Social Work	298
Religion	248

This book will help you decide whether graduate and professional school is something you want to pursue. It will also take you through all the steps of the admissions process for graduate and professional programs, including standardized tests, personal statements, letters of recommendation, interviews, and timelines for applying to various programs. In addition, the book will provide help in deciding which schools to apply to and then how to select a school after you have been admitted. Financial aid warrants a chapter of its own due to its importance to most applicants. The book concludes with an extensive resources section that tells you where to look for additional information on a variety of topics. You will find handy charts at key places in the book that you can use throughout your decision-making process.

chapter 2

Self-Assessment and Goals

Before you embark on the journey of graduate or professional school, you should spend a good amount of time questioning yourself about why you are going and whether it is the right choice for you. For those who choose it for the right reasons, graduate or professional school can be incredibly rewarding and fulfilling. Conversely, the experience can be quite painful, if once you get there, you realize that you don't know why you're there.

Chapter 1 listed some common reasons people give for going on to graduate and professional school. This chapter will help you to analyze those reasons, and decide whether any of them are valid for you; it will also provide information about the traits that are common for people who choose to get advanced degrees.

Although I spent most of my senior year of college thinking about whether I wanted to attend law school, once I arrived at law school, I was unhappy. I didn't enjoy the Socratic method, the large classes, or the generally competitive atmosphere. When I realized that most of my classmates wanted to work at large law firms and I found out what that involved, I really began to question my decision. Since I wasn't sure why I was there or what I hoped to gain from the experience, I took a leave of absence after my first year, assuming that I would never return. After two years of working and traveling, I decided that I did want to return to law school. Even though I still wasn't sure that I wanted to practice law, I knew enough about the world and about the law to recognize that having a law degree would better help me to understand legal issues that I was confronting in the work world and reading about in the newspaper. Returning to law school with a clearer vision of why I was there made the second and third years, while not fun, more bearable.

Common Reasons for Attending Graduate or Professional School

Perhaps you are thinking about graduate or professional school because a particular degree is required for the type of career you want to pursue (i.e., being a doctor or a lawyer). Although it may seem as if there are many careers that require a particular type of degree, if you look closely at the career, it may be that most people in that career have a certain degree but that the degree is not necessary. It's important to be realistic about presumed requirements. While you obviously need a law degree in order to practice law, you do not necessarily need an MBA in order to be in management at a company. You can also think about the entire field that you are considering entering. If you're thinking about law, for instance, you might decide that you would rather be a paralegal than a lawyer.

A good adviser can be a great help to you as you are trying to assess your reasons for getting a degree beyond a BA or BS., Your undergraduate career services office (many offices provide services for their alumni, as well) can help you assess yourself and your motivations and can help you make an informed decision about whether graduate or professional school is right for you.

Perhaps you are already working in a field and you want to advance in that field. You may have been told or you may know that you will be unable to do that without an advanced degree, no matter how talented you are. This is a good reason to continue your education, especially if you can get your employer to help you pay for it.

Maybe you want an advanced degree because it will provide you with a higher salary than you could obtain without it. This reason clearly has merit. The Census Bureau reports that over a 40-year career, those with bachelor's degrees will earn an average of $1,670,000. This is in stark contrast to those with professional degrees who can expect lifetime earnings of $3,280,000 and those with doctorates who will earn $2,640,000. Those with master's degrees can expect to earn only $250,000 more than those with bachelor's degrees.

If you are thinking about getting a graduate or professional degree solely because of the money, and you don't think you will like the profession you will have to enter, you might want to think about whether there are other ways you could earn that money. If you are unhappy in your career, you will most likely not be successful in it, which will diminish your earning potential. If you pick a career you like, you will be far more likely to make a good salary and be happy.

You may want to go to graduate school because you are interested in a particular field and want to study it in more depth. If this is your reason, you need to decide how much time you want to devote to pursuing this passion. You may have such a desire to learn that you want to get a PhD and spend your life teaching and continuing to learn about that field. Or you may decide that you want to get a master's degree because it will take only one or two years and will satisfy your urge to know more about an area. It might not matter to you whether you are able to continue working in that field. An alternative solution would be to use your free time to study the area that interests you on your own.

Some people work for a few years and find that they miss the intellectual challenge provided by school. Getting an advanced degree, especially a master's degree, can be a wonderful way to meet your intellectual needs. A master's degree can be good in this situation, because you can pursue it part-time while you continue to work. It also takes less time than any of the other degrees. You might be able to meet your intellectual needs by taking non-degree classes or by studying on your own.

Some schools offer a Master of Arts in Liberal Studies (MALS) degree, which is designed for working adults who want intellectual stimulation but who aren't necessarily looking to change jobs or to study one field in great depth. If a program like that would suit your needs, check with universities near you to see if they offer it.

You may be thinking that the job market is bad, and perhaps it won't be as bad when you graduate with an advanced degree. You may also reason that the advanced degree will make you more employable, even if the job market is still weak when you graduate. This reason needs to be analyzed very carefully. Any time there is a bad job market, there are still millions of people who are happily employed. It would be wise to look hard for a job before concluding that your only viable option is attending school. You shouldn't assume that having an advanced degree will make you more employable. It will simply change your career options and could substitute one bad job market for another. As discussed in Chapter 10 on job options, the teaching market for doctoral recipients is extremely weak right now, so having a PhD is no guarantee that you can get a job.

If you don't know what to do with your life, you may think that graduate or professional school is a perfect way to postpone that decision. Unfortunately, however, a postponement is all that it is. Once you receive your degree, you will still have to figure out what kind of job you want and where you want to work.

Additional Factors to Consider

Once you have thought about your reasons for pursuing an advanced degree, there are additional factors that you should consider including interest, time, money, support, and motivation.

You need to make sure that you are really interested in the field you plan to study. The thought of being a nuclear physicist may be exciting because you have always enjoyed science, but once you really think about what physicists do, you may decide that you would be better suited to a different career.

One way to determine your true interest in a field and to ensure that you understand what it involves, is to talk to a number of people who have degrees in the area you are considering. Ask them if they are happy or unhappy with their choices, and more importantly, ask them why. It could be that the job factors that they hate are the very ones that you will love. That's why you need to probe and not just accept superficial statements about how wonderful or horrible a particular job is. Try to get people to be very specific about the day-to-day activities in their jobs and imagine yourself performing those tasks.

Some people love the time they spend earning a graduate or professional degree and then find that they don't really like the career they get. Others hate school and love the career. You should try to consider both aspects of your experience. You may decide that you will enjoy school so much that you will worry about jobs once you graduate. In that case, you should recognize that it may take you more time and effort to find a job that satisfies you, because you won't want to follow the typical career path for people with your degree. The more common scenario is that people will decide to endure school so that they can get the ultimate reward of having the kind of job they like.

Frank was thinking about getting a Ph.D., so he talked to a professor at a state university. She said that she loved being able to spend lots of time doing research and she thrived in a "publish or perish" atmosphere. Frank wanted to teach because he was interested in students, so he thought perhaps a PhD wasn't the right path for him. He then talked to a professor at a liberal arts college who bemoaned the fact that he had to spend so much time teaching and interacting with students, because he wanted to devote himself to research. Frank realized that he was quite different from either of the professors to whom he spoke, but by listening to them and filtering what they said through his own values, he realized that he could find a spot for himself in teaching. He decided that he should try to find a position at a college where the emphasis would be on teaching rather than research.

You need to think seriously about whether you have the time, money, and energy needed to commit to a degree. If you go to graduate or professional school, you will be making a significant investment of these three major resources. You shouldn't make that decision lightly. You can learn about the kind of time and energy commitment that will be needed in Chapter 7 and about money in Chapter 8.

Keep in mind as you're making your plans that graduation is not the end for many programs. You may still have to pass a test to be licensed to practice in that area.

If you are married or have children, it is crucial that your family be supportive of your educational goals. If your family is not supportive, you may find it difficult or impossible to finish your degree.

If you are not married, you may want to look at your parents, siblings, and friends to see if they will support you. If anyone significant in your life opposes your desire to attend school, you should take that opposition into account in your plans. It doesn't need to stop you from going, but it can make you work harder to find a strong support system apart from that person.

Make sure that you are the one who wants to get the degree you are pursuing and you aren't doing it for a parent or someone else. It can be easy to confuse your motivations with theirs and not realize that you are really fulfilling your parents' desires.

Steve's father was an engineer who thoroughly enjoyed what he did. Steve was surrounded by engineers while he was growing up because his father often had his colleagues over. Since Steve had an aptitude for engineering and was very close to his father, he decided to pursue a master's degree in engineering. After he got his degree and had worked in the field for a few years, he recognized that he was not happy as an engineer. Without realizing it, he had become an engineer primarily because that was what his father was and he wanted his father's respect and admiration.

Traits to Consider

This section will talk about specific traits that it are common to many people who attend graduate or professional school. These traits will be important both in school and once you have graduated.

- First and foremost, you should be a high achiever who is used to demanding a lot of yourself. Your program will demand a lot of you, and if you have been used to meeting those demands in the past and excelling, you will continue that pattern in graduate and professional school.
- You should be well-organized. As you will see in Chapter 7, you will be given a great deal of material to study in school and will be expected to prioritize and figure out a way to accomplish all of your work.

- You should be self-motivated. You will be expected to assume the responsibility for much of your learning while in graduate and professional school. The most common reasons for people not finishing their doctoral theses is lack of motivation and procrastination. You will be expected to continue educating yourself once you have graduated, since you will have to stay on top of the most recent developments in your field.
- Clearly, you should be intelligent. The number of people who receive advanced degrees is relatively small and selective. You will be surrounded by many other intelligent people and will need to hold your own with them.
- You should have good analytical skills and be able to solve problems, using both logic and creativity.
- You should be able to tolerate uncertainty and frustration, especially if you are going to pursue medicine, law, or a research-oriented degree. In a research position, it's possible to spend years in a lab searching for a solution without ever finding it. In medicine and law, there are many gray areas, and you have to be able to deal with that ambiguity. You may not know if your proposed treatment is going to make your patient better or worse; you may not know whether the advice you give your client will be upheld in court.
- Since you'll have to do a lot of reading, you should have excellent reading abilities. This includes being able to read quickly and synthesize what you have read.
- If you are going into law or are pursuing an academic master's degree or a Ph.D., you should have good research skills and should like researching.
- If you are pursuing medicine or law or you plan to teach, you should have good oral communication skills. The ability to listen is also crucial, especially for lawyers and doctors. Your clients and patients may not always tell you everything, so you will have to listen closely for cues to know when to probe for more.

- If you're going to graduate school, you should enjoy studying independently. You need to have a keen understanding of the solitary nature of your work. Even though you will have colleagues and peers, you will spend a great deal of your time researching and writing alone. If you took an independent study class in college and didn't enjoy it or found it hard to stay motivated, an academic graduate degree might not be the right choice for you.
- Conversely, if you enjoy teamwork and being with other people, an MBA degree could be just the program for you. Teamwork is emphasized in MBA programs, since you will have to work with a wide variety of people when you are out working.
- Lawyers and doctors have to deal with people's emotional issues as well as their medical and legal issues, so it's important for you to be empathetic and understanding if you plan to pursue either of those two professions.
- If you're going to law school, you should have a strong interest in seeing that justice is done.

Gender and Ethnicity

A special word is in order here for women and people of color. Although great strides have been made, women and people of color are still underrepresented in almost all graduate and professional degree programs and in the careers that follow from those degrees. This should not dissuade you from getting those degrees, but it is something you should be aware of as you make your plans. This may mean that you will want to find a program that has a large number of students and faculty who are women and people of color.

You might decide that you want to be trailblazer and will choose a career because you want to be a role model for other people who are like you. This is noble and worthy. Just remember that you're the one who has to live your life, and being a trailblazer can grow old very quickly if you don't much care for what you are doing.

Prabha was smart and had always done well in science classes. Because of that, she received some encouragement to go to medical school. She thought it would be a good fit, and she was particularly interested in the fact that there weren't many women of color attending medical school. Once she enrolled, however, she realized that she didn't want to be a doctor. While she was good in science, she didn't like it that much and was finally able to admit to herself that her interests in writing were much stronger, and that she was as good at writing as she was at science.

Conclusion

Taking the time to seriously consider your interests, motivations, values, and strengths can help you tremendously as you decide whether you want to attend graduate or professional school and which program you want to pursue. Keep this chapter in mind as you read the rest of the book and get a better idea of what the different programs are like and what kinds of jobs you can get after you graduate. At the end of the book, you should reread this chapter and see what kind of response you have to this material at the point when you are far better informed about the process. That's when you can seriously analyze your situation and make the choice that's right for you.

Standardized Tests

If you're like most people, you probably started taking standardized tests in elementary school. The tests weren't fun, but the school saw them as a good way to compare you to your peers and to determine the quality of education at your particular school. Standardized tests are no more fun now than they were then, but they are used for similar purposes in the admissions process for graduate and professional schools. They give admissions officers additional information about you by providing an objective, standardized way to evaluate you against all of the others who are applying for the same program.

Applicants often ask why a score from a one-day standardized test should receive as much or more emphasis than their four years of hard work at an undergraduate institution. The answer is that although standardized tests are imperfect, they do provide some useful information to an admissions committee that is otherwise unobtainable. There is no way for an admissions committee to be intimately familiar with the rigor of every course in every major at every undergraduate institution in the country. A standardized test helps to provide an additional context for viewing your undergraduate grades.

Standardized tests also help to provide an indication of the quality of your undergraduate institution or the grading practices there. Suppose you have a 3.4 GPA at University A and are competing for admission to graduate school with someone who has a 3.6 from University B. The assumption is that the student from University B is stronger than you are. But, what if University B engages in grade inflation, so that the student at University B is only in the top half of the class there, while you are in the top 25 percent of the class at University A? You clearly would want the admissions committee to know that your school does not engage in grade inflation. A standardized test is one way for them to get that information. Thus, if you have a somewhat low GPA but a high standardized test score, the test score can indicate to an admissions committee that your school does not engage in grade inflation or that your school is very competitive, so that even though your grades were not at the top of the scale, you still are a worthy candidate.

Of course, your low grades and high test score can indicate other things to an admissions committee, too. At some schools, applicants who have a low undergraduate GPA and a high test score are called "bright goof-offs." These applicants can be very troubling for an admissions committee because the committee doesn't know whether your test score indicates that you are capable of doing the work and so the test score should be given more weight than your GPA or whether you are lazy and will continue to be so in graduate or professional school. If your grades and test score place you into this category, Chapter 5 will tell you more about how you can best present yourself to the admissions committee.

Whether you like standardized tests or not, they play an important role in the admissions process. Thus, you need to know how you can prepare for the tests and to have some general idea of what is covered in each test. Entire books have been written about each of the standardized tests, so this chapter will not attempt to duplicate that information. What you will find here is a good basic understanding of each of the standardized tests, including the Law School Admission Test (LSAT), the Graduate Management Admission Test (GMAT), the Medical College Admission Test (MCAT), and the Graduate Record Examination (GRE).

Preparation

As with all important events in your life, *preparation* is key when you are planning to take a standardized test . Whether you're taking an aptitude test or a skills test, there are ways you can get ready for it. You can be best prepared by becoming familiar with the types of questions that will be asked and learning how best to approach them.

Plan to spend time preparing for the test you intend to take.

There are two primary ways to study for a standardized test. One is to purchase materials from a bookstore or from the test provider and to study those materials on your own. The other is to take a test preparation course from a commercial test preparation company. Neither method is necessarily better than the other. What's most important is that you find the method that's best for you.

The most important factor is that you take the time to study for the test and that you are serious about it. Being serious includes taking at least three timed practice tests, so that you are completely comfortable with the nature of the test. One of the greatest obstacles for some test-takers is running out of time. You can help to alleviate this problem by knowing what to expect ahead of time.

One advantage of taking a commercial test preparation course is that since you are paying money for the course (and a lot of it!), you are more likely to study and be diligent about keeping up with it. You also will be studying with other people who can help provide additional motivation and inspiration. Finally, you are being taught by people who are successful at taking standardized tests who, presumably, can share some of their wisdom with you.

A possible disadvantage of a commercial test preparation course is that the people teaching you might be good at taking standardized tests, but they might have difficulty conveying their test-taking skills to you. Their success on standardized tests might just come naturally and they might not know how or why they do well on them. Commercial test preparation courses are also quite expensive, and when added to the cost of registering for the test and paying application fees at schools, the cost can be prohibitive.

Some of the more well-known test preparation companies are The Princeton Review and Kaplan. Both of these companies are well-established and have been around for some time. They both offer preparation courses for all of the standardized tests. Other companies that offer test preparation courses may specialize just in the test you plan to take. If you are seriously considering taking a test preparation course, you should shop around and look at more than one company. Ask about the background and training of the instructors at the location where you will be taking the course. Ask about cost and whether the company will give you your money back if you don't achieve a certain percentage increase in your score from when you first started taking the course. Some test preparation companies also offer discounts on the registration fee for needy applicants.

A common statement made by applicants is, "I was consistently scoring in the 90th–95th percentile when I took the practice tests, but when I took the real test, I only scored in the 75th percentile." Beware that practice tests might not be a completely accurate predictor of how well you will do on the actual test.

As long as you put in the time, you can learn just as much from your own studies as you can from a commercial preparation course. Since you would not be considering graduate or professional school unless you were highly motivated and prepared to work hard there, finding the motivation and discipline to study on your own should not be too hard. If you find that it is too difficult, that might be a good sign for you to consider whether graduate or professional school is really the right path to take.

If you are going to prepare for the test on your own, you should first contact the company that administers the test you plan to take and find out what test preparation materials they provide (addresses are listed in Chapter 11). Usually these materials are provided for a fee. Since they are produced by the same people who administer the test, they are usually a great source of information. Other test preparation guides are available at bookstores. There is a wide variety of resources from which to choose, including some CD-ROM products. Some of the big names in this area are *Barron's*, *Arco*, *Kaplan*, and *Princeton Review*.

Shortly before the test, you should make sure that you know the exact location where the test will be held. If you haven't been to that location before, you might want to drive there ahead of time just so you know how to get there. The night before the test is not a good time to go out drinking (save that for the night *after* the test). Make sure you get plenty of sleep.

On the morning of the test, set your alarm, have a friend call you, or do whatever is necessary to make sure that you get up in plenty of time to get to the test. You should eat a good breakfast, take several sharpened pencils, and make sure you have the admission documents sent to you by the testing agency and a photo ID. Since you will be at the test site anywhere from three to seven hours, you might take a snack that you can eat during one of your breaks. Getting some food into your system can keep your energy level and concentration high. You should also plan to arrive at the testing site early.

On the morning of the Medical College Admission Test, Kathy arrived early at the testing center, only to find out that they had changed her test center to another center 30 minutes away. Since she was so early, she was able to drive to the second test center in enough time to register and take the test on time. Although she was understandably distressed, she was happy that she was still able to take the test.

If you have a tendency to panic while you are taking standardized tests, try to find ways to remain calm and relaxed during the test.

While you are taking the test, you might follow some of these tips to help you get through it:

- Read each question carefully and read each answer before you select one. Although you may think that "A" is the right answer, you can't be sure until you have read the other choices. "A" may be a good answer, but it may not be the best answer to that question.
- Follow the directions very carefully.
- Don't get distracted by the proctor, your growling stomach, someone being noisy next to you, or anything else. Stay focused on the test.
- Pace yourself during the test to make sure that you use your time effectively and well. There is no reward for finishing early, there is a big penalty for not finishing the test and not answering all of the questions.

If you have a disability, you should contact the testing agency to find out what types of accommodations they will offer. Generally, they will require documentation of your disability and the type of accommodation you are requesting.

When to Take a Test

Typically, you should plan to take a standardized test in the summer or fall of the year prior to when you plan to start school (nine to 15 months before beginning graduate or professional school). This requires planning and means that you generally cannot wait until the summer before you want to start school and then try to take a standardized test and apply for that fall.

Take a standardized test at least 9–15 months before you expect to begin school.

Schools will generally accept scores for three to five years after they were earned, so it is possible to take a test and then not apply immediately to graduate or professional school. An advantage to taking the test while you are still an undergraduate or just after you have graduated is that you are still familiar with tests and test-taking strategies that may help you perform better than if you wait until you have been away from the academic, test-taking world for a period of time. Of course, if you aren't sure which graduate or professional degree you wish to pursue or you don't think you will apply to schools during the next five years, you should wait to take the test until closer to the time when you plan to apply.

Retaking a Standardized Test

Most schools will average your scores if you take a standardized test more than once, although this can vary from test to test and school to school. It is best not to take a "real" test as a practice test, since there is a high likelihood that at least one of the schools to which you will apply will count both the first score and the second score. Even if schools don't actually consider your first score, it will be given to them along with your second score, and it doesn't help your application to have a low first score.

Plan to take a standardized test only once.

If you take a test and are not happy with your score, you have to decide whether you want to retake the test. Depending on the program to which you are applying and the type of test you are taking, you may be able to take the test a second time and still be able to apply for the following year. In other cases, you will have to wait for another year to apply to school. If you are considering retaking the test, you should check with the schools to which you want to apply to find out whether you still have time to retake the test and apply for that year.

George took the Law School Admission Test in December and was very unhappy with the score he received. He wanted to apply to attend law school for the following September. He found out that the next time the Law School Admission Test was offered was in February and very few law schools would consider his score from the February administration. He decided not to retake the test, because he didn't want to postpone law school for a year.

Most of the testing agencies encourage applicants to think carefully about retaking a standardized test. Unless there is some specific reason why you think that you did not do well on the standardized test the first time you took it, it probably doesn't pay to take it again. Your score may not improve, and in fact, it may decline. Law Services, the agency that administers the Law School Admission Test, provides test-repeater data in its information, so you can look and see the likelihood of your score improving.

If you are sick on the day of the test, you should check the information you have from the testing agency to find out what procedure to follow. Most of them will give you a telephone number you can call and will allow you to reschedule the test for a later date, sometimes for an additional fee.

Fee Waivers

The fees charged for standardized tests range from $84.00 for the Law School Admission Test to $125.00 for the Graduate Management Admission Test. Additional fees are charged if you wish to test outside of the United States or for late registration or other services. No matter which test you take, it will not be cheap. This can be a real burden for those who are not well off financially.

Fortunately, all standardized test administrators offer a fee waiver service for those who cannot afford to pay for the test. Some even will provide free test preparation materials to you if they have granted you a fee waiver. If you feel that you cannot afford the registration fee for a standardized test, be sure to contact the test administrator to inquire about the fee waiver program. At a minimum, you will be required to provide proof of income.

Test-taker Misconduct

This may seem obvious, but it bears mentioning here. If you don't follow the rules given to you by the testing agency in advance of the test or the proctors during the test, you will have to suffer the consequences. For example, if you're taking a paper-based test and you finish one section, you can't go on to the next section until the proctor tells you it's okay to do so. If you do engage in some form of misconduct, you may be kicked out of the test or your score may be invalidated. If you use common sense and pay attention to the directions that are given, you will make sure that you do not get into trouble.

Testing Irregularities

Despite the best efforts of the testing agencies, irregularities sometimes occur in the administration of a standardized test. Recently, one of the tests started two hours after the stated starting time due to problems with the proctors. Your test also might be disturbed because of loud construction noise going on outside the building, a fire alarm being set off, or someone getting sick in the seat next to you. If these irregularities occur, you should make sure to contact the testing agency to find out what remedy they will offer. They will usually give you the choice to have your score reported to the schools with an explanation of the irregularity that occurred while you were taking the test or of retaking the test at a later date at no charge.

Now that you know some general information about taking standardized tests for graduate and professional school and how to prepare for them, you need to know some specifics about each of the tests. If you already know which test you want to take, you can simply skip to that section. If you are curious about all of the tests, you can read every section. As you would expect, there are similarities and differences among the various tests. The most important difference, which will be covered in detail later in this chapter, is that some tests are offered as computer-based tests, while others are offered as the traditional paper-based tests.

Law School Admission Test (LSAT)

All ABA (American Bar Association)-approved law schools require you to take the Law School Admission Test (LSAT) as a condition of admission. The LSAT is designed to measure your ability to do well during the first year of law school, particularly your ability to read and understand complicated texts; to draw inferences from information that is presented to you; and to use critical reasoning skills. The LSAT is an aptitude test and is not designed to test knowledge of specific subjects.

LSAT is a four-hour test that is designed to be a predictor of your performance during your first year of law school. The test has five 35-minute sections with multiple-choice questions and a 30-minute writing sample. Four of the five multiple-choice sections are scored, while the fifth is used to pretest new test items. The writing sample is not scored but is sent to law schools in its entirety, along with your LSAT score. The test is offered four times a year (June, October, December, and February) and is currently offered only as a paper test. Plans for a computerized test are under way but probably will not be operational for a number of years.

The vast majority of test-takers take the LSAT in October and plan to apply to law schools that year to start the following fall. If you can manage to fit it into your schedule, it is a good idea to take the test in June, since then you have a second good opportunity to take the test if you get sick on the June test date or something else unforeseen happens. Although law schools will accept scores from the December test for admission for the following fall, you are placing yourself at a competitive disadvantage in the admissions process if you take the December test.

If possible, plan to take the LSAT in June 15 months prior to when you would start law school.

The minimum score on the LSAT is 120; the maximum is 180. Approximately 70 percent of test-takers will receive a score between 140 and 160. This means that the middle of the scale is tightly compressed and there are fewer people at the lower and higher ends of the scale. From the early 1980s to 1991, the scale was 10–48; prior to that, it was 200–800. The score scale has continued to change as Law Services has tried to make the test more precise and accurate.

> Law Services has released statistics that show the preparation method of choice for the LSAT high scorers is to purchase the preparation materials produced by Law Services and to work through them while timing yourself.

The cost of the LSAT is $84.00. In addition, almost all law schools require applicants to subscribe to the Law School Data Assembly Service (LSDAS). This service is provided by Law Services. Most applicants register for the LSDAS at the same time that they register for the LSAT, although this is not required. The LSDAS prepares a report that contains your LSAT score, a copy of your writing sample, copies of all of your undergraduate and graduate transcripts, and a summary sheet that provides additional information to the law schools.

This summary sheet shows your transcript in a version that has been converted by Law Services. This conversion is done to make all grading scales equivalent. Since it is difficult for law schools to compare grades earned on a seven-point scale to those earned on a four-point scale, Law Services has adopted a uniform system that accounts for these differences.

You do not tell Law Services which schools should receive your reports. Once you apply to a school, that school requests your report from Law Services and it is automatically sent to the school. However, since you have to pay for each report sent by Law Services, you should have some idea of how many schools you'll be applying to, so you'll know how many to pay for. The basic cost for the LSDAS is $85.00, which includes one law school report. Each additional report costs $8.00 at the time of your initial LSDAS registration. If you decide later that you want more schools to be able to receive your report, the cost for each additional report is $10.00.

When you register for the LSAT or subscribe to the LSDAS, you can give Law Services permission to give information about you to law schools before you apply. This is known as the Candidate Referral Service, or CRS. Schools will send a request to Law Services to identify students with certain characteristics (having a certain GPA or LSAT score, being from a particular area of the country, or others) and will receive names and addresses of applicants meeting those criteria. The schools will then send a mailing to the applicants encouraging them to apply to their school. There is no cost to you to register for the CRS, and you may consider schools that you wouldn't have thought about otherwise.

As mentioned before there are five sections of multiple-choice questions on the LSAT. Four of these sections are scored, while the fifth is used to pretest new test items. You will not know when you are taking the test which is the "experimental" section. Each test will have only three types of questions. They are logical reasoning, reading comprehension, and analytical reasoning.

Logical Reasoning

Two of the sections consist of logical reasoning questions or arguments. In these sections you will read a short passage of about 100 words and then be asked to respond to one or two questions about it. This is not the same as the reading comprehension section, which you may be familiar with from other standardized tests. The difference is that the logical reasoning passage will contain some type of argument, and the question will relate to that argument. The questions will test your ability to reason logically. You do not need to have taken a logic class or to be familiar with specialized terms relating to logic.

In the logical reasoning sections, you may have to find errors in reasoning, draw a conclusion from the evidence given, state the assumptions used in a line of reasoning, figure out how more evidence might affect the outcome of an argument, or articulate the point of an argument.

Reading Comprehension

This section is similar to other reading comprehension tests you have taken. You will read four passages of approximately 450 words that will be followed by six to eight questions designed to test your understanding of the material you have read. The reading comprehension passages are taken from a wide variety of subject matter and do not assume familiarity with any particular field of knowledge.

When reading these passages, it may be helpful for you to underline key sections or make quick notes in the margin that you can refer back to when you are answering the questions. You may find that it is most effective for you to read the passage very carefully first and then answer the questions. Alternatively, you might want to skim the passage and the questions so you have some idea of what to look for while you are reading the material. Then you can go back and read the passage very carefully. A third alternative is to read the questions first, then read the passage very carefully, and then answer the questions.

Analytical Reasoning

A section of the LSAT that appeals to people who like puzzles, games, or brain teasers is called analytical reasoning. This section is often referred to as the "games" section. You are given a set of conditions and then are asked to draw conclusions based on those conditions. The section contains four sets of conditions and five to seven questions about each set of conditions.

An example of this type of question might be the following:

> Four children named Vanessa, Ralph, Megan, and Paul each want a different present for Christmas. One wants a TV, one wants a dog, another wants a computer, and the fourth wants a phone. The children's last names are Smith, Jones, Klein, and Gordon. Based on the following clues, you must match the first and last names and the present each one wants.
>
> > Smith wants her present delivered on Christmas Eve so she can call her friends.
> >
> > Ralph wants his present unwrapped and with air holes.
> >
> > Jones wants to watch her present.
> >
> > Vanessa does not want to open her present on Christmas Eve.
> >
> > Gordon already has a computer.

Writing Sample

For the writing sample, you will be provided with a factual situation with two suggested outcomes, and you will be asked to choose one of the outcomes and to explain why it is the better one. An abbreviated example of this type of question might be:

> A small town in Iowa needs to find a new general practitioner to replace the one who is retiring. They have interviewed Dr. Leslie Bates and Dr. Gregory Jones and have to decide between them. Dr. Bates has worked in a small town before, but there is some question about her bedside manner and how well she treats patients. Dr. Jones says that he is looking to move out of the city, but he has never lived in a rural location before. Which doctor should the town choose and why?

Admissions committees are looking for evidence of clear writing that is free of grammatical errors. They are also looking to see your thought processes and how well you can defend a particular position. Use of the writing sample in the admissions process varies greatly from school to school. It is read primarily when there is a question about your writing ability (perhaps you are a science or engineering major and did not take many writing classes) or the committee is on the fence about your file and is looking for extra evidence that can tip the balance one way or the other.

Graduate Management Admission Test (GMAT)

The GMAT is sponsored by the Graduate Management Admission Council (GMAC) and is administered by Educational Testing Service (ETS). It is required by about 850 graduate management programs and is accepted and used by an additional 450 programs. Like the LSAT, the GMAT is an aptitude test; it measures general verbal, mathematical, and analytical writing skills. It does not test for specific knowledge of business or any other subject matter. It is designed to be a useful predictor of your performance during your first year of business school.

In October 1997, the GMAT began to be administered as a computer-adaptive test (CAT) in North America and many other countries, although in some countries, it is still only offered as a paper test. Where the CAT is offered, that is the only format that can be used. Thus, you are not able to choose between a paper-based test and a CAT. In a CAT, you will see one question at a time on a computer screen. The first question will be of medium difficulty, and your response to that question will determine subsequent questions. The questions are selected randomly from a large pool of questions of similar difficulty and are always gauged to your level of ability. The idea is that you should not get too many questions that are either too difficult or too easy for you to answer.

One of the advantages of the GMAT CAT is that you have much more flexibility as to when you can take the exam. The exam is available six days a week, for three weeks per month, throughout the year. You simply call and select a date of your choice. You will receive your test results approximately two weeks after you take the test. You are able to retake the test once every calendar month. The last three scores you receive will be sent to the business schools. Since you have so much flexibility in scheduling the test, you should plan to take it when it will best fit into your schedule and when you think you can do the best on it.

The GMAT is a four-hour test that is designed to predict your performance during your first year of business school. The test has five sections of multiple-choice questions and two essay-writing sections. The five sections of multiple-choice questions are divided into two general categories: quantitative and verbal. The quantitative part of the test has two sections. One is basic problem solving, and the other is data sufficiency. The verbal part of the test has three sections: reading comprehension, critical reasoning, and sentence correction.

You will receive four scores after you take the GMAT. The most important score is the overall multiple-choice score that covers all five of the multiple choice sections. The minimum overall score is 200, and the maximum score is 800. An average score on the test is 500. You will also receive a score just for the verbal part of the test and another score just for the quantitative part of the test. Unless a school is very quantitatively oriented, it probably will not look very closely at your quantitative score but only at your overall score. Schools will look closely at verbal scores primarily if the applicant is not a native English speaker.

The fourth score you will receive is based upon the two essays you write for the GMAT. You'll receive one score for both essays. The minimum score is 0 and the maximum score is 6. Scores are reported in half-point increments; the average score is 3.5. Schools will receive copies of the essays and can choose to read them if they wish.

The GMAT costs $125.00 if you take it in the United States, U.S. territories, or Puerto Rico. It costs more if you take it overseas. This fee includes sending your score reports to five schools. If you wish to apply to more than five schools, each additional score report costs $15.00. You tell ETS which schools you wish to receive your test score reports. They will send reports only to those schools.

As part of the registration process for the GMAT, you are automatically registered for the Graduate Management Admission Search Service (GMASS). This service attempts to match you with schools who are seeking students with your characteristics. GMASS will give the schools your name and address, and the schools will then send you literature encouraging you apply. If you do not wish to be included in GMASS, you must write to

GMASS, P.O. Box 6109, Princeton, NJ 08541-6109, and ask to be removed from the GMASS mailing list.

Now that you understand some general information about the GMAT, you will want to know something about each of the specific sections covered in the test. You can find that information in the following paragraphs.

Verbal Section

In the verbal section, you will have 75 minutes to answer 41 questions. This section measures your ability to understand and evaluate what you have read and your ability to recognize basic conventions of standard written English. Reading comprehension, critical reasoning, and sentence correction questions will be mingled within the verbal section.

Reading Comprehension

The reading comprehension questions you will get are quite similar to the reading comprehension portion of the LSAT and other standardized tests you have taken. You will be given a relatively long passage to read and then will be asked questions that will demonstrate how well you understand what you read.

Critical Reasoning

The critical reasoning questions on the test are similar to the logical reasoning questions on the LSAT. You will be given a short passage to read and then will be asked questions about that passage. The types of questions you will be asked will measure your ability to understand an argument that is being made and to reason about conclusions that can be drawn from that argument.

Sentence Correction

The sentence correction questions will give you a sentence that is partially underlined. You will then be given four other ways that the underlined part of the sentence could be written. You have to choose the answer forming the most grammatically correct sentence containing no ambiguity or awkwardness.

Quantitative Section

The quantitative section gives you 75 minutes to respond to 37 questions. This section measures your basic mathematical skills and your understanding of elementary concepts. It also measures your ability to interpret graphical data, reason quantitatively, and solve quantitative problems. Problem solving and data sufficiency questions will be mingled within the quantitative section.

Problem Solving

Remember those word problems you used to get in math class? They're back in a more sophisticated manner on the GMAT. For these questions, you are given a math problem that is expressed in words and asked to compute the correct numerical answer.

Data Sufficiency

Data sufficiency problems have a question and two statements that give you certain data. You have to determine whether the data given in the statements is sufficient to answer the questions. You will choose from five answers for each question. They are:

- The first statement is sufficient to answer the question by itself, but the second statement is not sufficient to answer the question by itself.
- The second statement is sufficient to answer the question by itself, but the first statement is not sufficient to answer the question by itself.
- Both statements together are sufficient to answer the question, but neither statement alone is sufficient.
- Each statement alone is sufficient to answer the question.
- Both statements together are not sufficient to answer the question and additional data is needed.

Analytical Writing

The analytical writing section of the test consists of two essays that you will be asked to write. You will have 30 minutes to write each essay. In one of the essays, you will be asked to analyze an argument. In the other, you will be asked to analyze an issue. Your essays will be scored based on how well you use standard English, whether you provide good supporting arguments for your response, and how well you organize, develop, and express your thoughts.

Analysis of an Argument

In the analysis of an argument section, you will be given a brief argument to read. You will then be asked to evaluate the validity of the position being advanced by the writer in terms of how well she or he has presented the argument. You will need to look at what the writer is actually arguing and how well she or he presents that argument in terms of reasoning ability and the use of evidence to support the argument. You are not being asked to write what you think about the topic.

Analysis of an Issue

In the analysis of an issue section, you will be asked for your response to an issue that is presented to you. There is no right or wrong answer to the issue. This section measures your ability to communicate complex ideas through writing and to think critically. The LSAT writing sample question provided on page ___ is a good example of the type of question you might be asked in this section of the GMAT.

Medical College Admission Test (MCAT)

Almost all American medical schools require the MCAT for admission. This is a multiple-choice test that is an aptitude test like the LSAT and GMAT in that it assesses problem solving, critical thinking, and writing skills, but it is also a skills test in that it tests specific knowledge of science concepts and principles that are prerequisite to the study of medicine.

It is recommended that people taking the MCAT have the equivalent of one year of college biology, general and/or inorganic chemistry, physics, and organic chemistry. A knowledge of calculus is not required. Generally, the equivalent of one year of college math or a strong background in high school math that includes algebra, geometry, and trigonometry should be sufficient.

The MCAT is a test of your thinking and analytical reasoning skills more than it is a test of how much science you actually know. Admissions committees can look at your college grades from your science classes to see how well you have done substantively. What they are looking for from the MCAT is your ability to think abstractly or to take ideas you know from a familiar context and apply them to a new context.

The MCAT gives you a way to help mitigate poor college grades. If you did poorly in biology, for example, and do well on the biological sciences portion of the MCAT, that might help the admissions committee overlook your poor performance in biology.

The MCAT is the longest standardized test required for admission to graduate or professional school. It lasts for a whopping six hours, plus you get an additional hour for lunch, so you should plan to be there for at least seven hours on the day of the test. The MCAT is produced by the Association of American Medical Colleges (AAMC) but is actually administered by American College Testing (ACT) located in Iowa City, Iowa. To register for the test, you contact ACT, but to get study materials for the test, you contact AAMC. Addresses for both are listed in Chapter 11.

The test is offered only twice a year: in April and in August. It is strongly recommended that applicants take the April exam, because it is best to apply for medical school in the summer, one year before you plan to begin your studies. If you wait until August to take the test, you may find yourself at a competitive disadvantage in the admissions process. Also, since the test is only offered twice a year, if you get sick or something precludes you from taking the test in August, you will be forced to wait an entire year before you can apply to medical school.

Because the MCAT is offered only twice a year, you should plan to take the test in April at the earliest administration.

The MCAT consists of four sections: verbal reasoning, physical sciences, writing samples, and biological sciences. You will receive four separate scores on the test, one for each section. The verbal reasoning, physical sciences, and biological sciences all have the same score scale. The minimum score is 1, and the maximum score is 15. Most admissions officers agree that you will not be considered for admission if you get below a 7 on any of the sections. Scores of 10 or above are usually competitive for admission. On the writing sample, you will receive a score that will actually be a letter from J (the lowest score) to T (the highest score). If you get between an N and a T, you have probably done well on that section.

The verbal reasoning section has 65 questions and lasts for 1 hour and 25 minutes. The physical sciences section has 77 questions that must be answered in 1 hour and 40 minutes. This section covers physics and chemistry. The biological sciences section also has 77 questions and lasts for 1 hour and 40 minutes. It covers biology and organic chemistry. There are two writing sample questions, each lasting 30 minutes. The next sections will cover each of these sections in turn.

Verbal Reasoning

We've covered this one before. It's very similar to the reading comprehension sections of the other standardized tests that this chapter has explored. The main difference is that the reading passages you will see on the MCAT will have an emphasis on the social sciences and the natural sciences with some humanities thrown in. In this section, you will be asked to read 9–10 passages. Each passage will be followed by 6–10 questions.

Physical Sciences

In the physical sciences section, you will be given 10–11 passages that will be followed by 6–10 multiple choice questions for each passage. The passages will be scientific in nature and may include data, the results of research, scientific, journal, or scholarly articles. Whereas in the verbal reasoning section, you are being asked to look at the structure and meaning of a passage, in the physical sciences section, you will have to understand the data in order to be able to extract information from it and apply it to the questions that are asked. In addition to these passages, you will also be given 10–15 problems that are not related to the passages. Each problem will have just one question. The questions in this section will be about evenly divided between physics and inorganic chemistry.

Biological Sciences

The biological sciences section follows the same format as the physical sciences section in terms of the number and types of questions you will be asked. The difference is that the subject matter of this section will be biology and organic chemistry. About 60 percent of the questions will be related to biology and about 40 percent will concern organic chemistry. For both the physical sciences and the biological sciences sections you will be given a periodic table of elements that you can refer to during the test.

Essays

For this portion of the test, you will be given two very short statements and asked to write an essay about each one of them. This statement might be something like, "Capitalism forms the basis for all good societies." In the essay, you will be asked to do three things. First, you will need to provide an explanation of the meaning of the passage. Second, you will have to give a concrete example that shows a point of view directly opposite to the viewpoint expressed in the statement you are given. Finally, you will have to explain how it is possible to resolve the conflict between the statement you have been given and the example you have given that is opposite to the statement. Each essay will be read and scored by two people, and the four scores will be combined to come up with the letter score you will receive.

Preparing for the MCAT in a comprehensive, planned way may be more important than preparing for any of the other standardized tests—for two reasons. One, a great deal of emphasis is placed on the MCAT in the admissions process. Two, because the MCAT is a skills test, you can study specific scientific concepts that will be tested on the exam. Many college juniors spend most of their waking hours outside of class studying for the MCAT.

Graduate Record Examination (GRE)

Many, although not all, graduate schools, require applicants to take the Graduate Record Examination (GRE). The weight placed on the GRE by admissions committees varies tremendously from school to school. Some consider the test scores to be very important, while others do not weigh them very heavily. You receive a score for each of the three sections of the general test. Some schools will weigh all three scores equally, while others will place more emphasis on two of the three scores. Schools' policies regarding the GRE and how it is used in the admissions process should be contained in their admissions materials. If they are not, ask the school.

Some schools might require you to take another test in addition to or instead of the GRE. That test is the Miller Analogies Test (MAT). It contains about 100 analogy problems and is designed to test your thinking skills.

There are two types of GRE tests. One is a *general test,* an aptitude test that measures general quantitative, verbal, and analytical skills. Because it is an aptitude test, it is not related to any particular field of study. The other is a *subject test* that measures achievement in a particular subject area. To do well on a subject test, you must have an extensive background in or knowledge of the subject matter being tested. Subject tests generally cover the kinds of knowledge you would have learned while taking a typical undergraduate curriculum in that field.

Depending on the graduate degree you pursue, you may be required to take the general test and a subject test, or you may only have to take the general test. It is very important to check with the schools that interest you to determine their requirements for test scores. Scores on both tests may be reported to schools for five years.

General Test

Like the GMAT, the GRE General Test is now offered as a computer-adaptive test. Unlike the GMAT, however, you still have the option to take the new computer test or the traditional paper test. Like with the GMAT, the computer-based test (CBT) can be scheduled year-round in a number of different testing centers, so it is easier to schedule it to meet your needs. The CBT can be scheduled during the first three weeks of the month from September through February and for the first two weeks of the month from March through August. The CBT contains fewer questions than the paper-based test, and the questions are tailored to your ability level. With the CBT, you may see your scores immediately upon completion of the test and can then choose four schools to receive those scores.

The CBT can last for up to four and a half hours. Only two hours and 15 minutes are used to answer questions that count toward your score. The rest of the time is spent on tutorials for those unfamiliar with using a computer or a mouse; background information questions; pretest and/or research sections; and a survey.

The paper version of the GRE lasts for three and a half hours of testing time. The test has seven sections, each of which lasts 30 minutes. One of the sections is used to pretest or research questions for future administrations, so answers to that section do not count towards your score.

You will receive three scores on the GRE General Test, one score for each of the three sections of the test (verbal, quantitative, and analytical ability). The minimum score for each of the sections is 200. The maximum score is 800.

The cost of the GRE General Test is $96.00 if you take it in the United States, U.S. territories, or Puerto Rico. This includes score reports being sent to four graduate schools. The cost for each additional score report is $13.00. Score reports will only be sent to the schools you designate.

ETS offers a free GRE Search Service. This service matches prospective students with graduate schools that are interested in someone with their qualifications. You can register for this service even if you have just begun tentatively thinking about graduate school and have not yet taken or even registered for the GRE. Participating schools will get your name and address from ETS and then will send you a letter telling you about their schools.

The paper-based General Test is only offered in November and April. It takes approximately six weeks to receive your scores when you take the paper-based test.

The GRE General Test has many components. The analytical ability section has questions on analytical and logical reasoning. The verbal ability section includes questions on reading comprehension, analogies, sentence completions, and antonyms. The quantitative section has questions on problem-solving and quantitative comparison. We'll cover each of these topics in turn.

Analytical Ability

Questions relating to analytical ability are designed to test how well you can think logically, in both formal and informal ways. Each question will be based on a table, passage, graph, or set of conditions. You will get questions that will test your ability to reason both analytically and logically.

Analytical Reasoning

The analytical reasoning section of the GRE General Test is much like the analytical reasoning section of the LSAT. See page ___ for a description of what is covered in this section and a sample question.

Logical Reasoning

The logical reasoning section of the GRE General Test is much like the logical reasoning section of the LSAT. See page ___ for a description of what is covered in this section.

Verbal Ability

Verbal ability questions measure your ability to solve problems by reasoning with words. To do this, you must be able to read, analyze, and comprehend relationships among words, sentences, and paragraphs. This section will include questions on reading comprehension, analogies, sentence completions, and antonyms.

Reading Comprehension

The reading comprehension section of the GRE General Test is quite similar to the reading comprehension sections of the LSAT and the GMAT. You will be given a long passage and then will be asked questions that are designed to test your understanding of that passage.

Analogies

In the analogy section, you will be given a word pair and will have to analyze the relationship between the two words. The word pair is the "question." The possible answers are five other word pairs. You have to determine which of those five word pairs has the closest relationship to the one expressed in the "question" word pair.

Sentence Completions

This section will give you a sentence that has two words missing from different parts of the sentence. You will be given five pairs of words that could be used to complete the sentence. Your task is to find the pair that best completes the sentence and makes it grammatically correct and logical.

Antonyms

In the antonym section you will be given a word and then will have five choices of other words or phrases. You will be asked to choose the word or phrase that is the most opposite to the initial word you were given.

Quantitative Ability

The quantitative questions on the GRE General Test measure your mathematical abilities in a variety of ways. To answer the questions, you would be expected to know high school–level math: arithmetic, geometry, algebra, and data analysis (statistics and interpreting graphs and tables are examples here).

You will be asked both problem-solving and quantitative comparison questions.

Problem Solving

Problem-solving questions require you to solve mathematical problems. They may be word problems, or they may be problems that require you to analyze graphs, charts, or tables of data. These are multiple-choice questions, so if you can get close to the answer, you can guess based on the answers provided.

Quantitative Comparison

In this section, you will be given two columns, A and B, each of which lists a quantity. You have to determine whether Quantity A is greater, whether Quantity B is greater, whether the quantities are equal, or whether the relationship between them can't be determined because you weren't given enough information.

Subject Test

The GRE Subject Test is only offered as a paper-based test. It is offered in 16 different subject matter areas and lasts for appxroximately three hours. ETS offers Subject Test Descriptive Booklets for each subject matter area. They contain sample test questions and test-taking strategies, and they describe the content of the test. You may obtain these free of charge. See Chapter 11 for contact information.

The minimum score for a Subject Test is 200, and the maximum score is 990. For some Subject Tests, you will also receive subscores, which range from 20 to 99.

Subject Tests are offered in November, December, and April, although not all Subject Tests are offered in November.

The following table lists all of the subject matter tests that are offered by ETS. Just because a subject test is offered in the area you want to study doesn't mean that you have to take that test. It is important for you to check with the schools to which you intend to apply to find out if they require a subject test.

GRE Subject Tests
Biochemistry, Cell, and Molecular Biology
Biology
Chemistry
Computer Science
Economics
Engineering
Geology
History
Literature in English
Mathematics
Music
Physics
Psychology
Sociology

Since you may be wondering what the subject tests are like, some brief information about them is included below. As you will see, the tests vary widely, from the number of questions asked to the types of questions that are asked.

Biochemistry, Cell, and Molecular Biology

Approximately 180 questions are included in this test. About 36 percent of the questions concern biochemistry, 28 percent relate to biology, and 36 percent concern molecular biology and genetics. The test may be required for programs in microbiology and genetics in addition to biochemistry, cell biology, and molecular biology.

Biology

This subject test has about 200 questions that are equally divided between cellular and molecular biology, organismal biology, and ecology and evolution.

Chemistry

About 15 percent of the 136 questions in the chemistry test are about analytical chemistry, 25 percent are about inorganic chemistry, 30 percent are about organic chemistry, and 30 percent are about physical chemistry. You should be able to answer the questions based on the chemistry courses you have taken by the first semester of your senior year in college.

Computer Science

The computer science test is designed for students who have majored in computer science or who have taken an equivalent number of computer science courses. This is one of the shortest tests, with only 70 questions. Approximately 35 percent of the questions relate to software systems and methodology, 20 percent concern computer organization and architecture, 25 percent are about theory, 15 percent are on mathematical background, and 5 percent relate to artificial intelligence, modeling, and simulation.

Economics

The economics test is designed to evaluate your understanding of basic economic analysis. The major portion of the test (about 60 percent) is divided between macroeconomic and microeconomic analysis. The next major portion of the test (33 percent) asks questions about other areas of economics including finance, law and economics, international economics, development, comparative systems, history of thought, urban and regional economics, and industrial organization. The final 7 percent of the test asks about basic statistics. There are 130 questions on this test.

Engineering

The engineering test has two subscores. One is for engineering and the other is for mathematics. The engineering component of the test is much larger and has about 105 questions. The mathematics portion of the test has only about 35 questions. You should be able to answer the engineering questions if you have completed the first two years of an engineering curriculum. The following areas are emphasized: basic physics and chemistry, mechanics, electric circuits and devices, fluid mechanics, and thermodynamics. The mathematics questions measure your ability to use mathematics in engineering and cover calculus.

Geology

The geology test has three subscores in the areas of stratigraphy and sedimentology, structural geology and tectonics, and mineralogy and petrology. Approximately 60 percent of the questions are in these three areas. The other 40 percent of the questions are divided as follows: geophysics (8 percent), surficial processes/geomorphology (6 percent), paleontology (8 percent), general geology (8 percent), and hydrogeology (10 percent). Answers to these 40 percent of the questions are used in calculating your overall score but are not used for any of your subscores. The test is designed to cover topics that should be included in your core geology courses.

History

Your two subscores on the history test will be on United States history and European history. About 50 percent of the questions are about general European history from ancient times to the present. About 35 percent of the questions are about U.S. history from the colonial period to the present. The rest of the questions (about 15 percent) ask about the history of other parts of the world and ask for comparisons to U.S. and European history.

Literature in English

This test has 230 questions—more questions than any of the other tests. The subject covered will be literature in English from the United States, England, and other countries. You will have interpretive questions and factual questions. The interpretive questions will measure your ability to read different types of passages and respond to questions about them. The factual questions will be about specific writers or written works that you should have studied in college.

Mathematics

This test has the fewest number of questions of all of the tests—only 66. The major portion of the test (about 75 percent) will ask questions relating to calculus, abstract algebra, real analysis, and linear algebra. You may be asked to create counterexamples and to prove theorems. The other 25 percent of the questions will relate to combinatorics, number theory, algorithmic processes, topology, probability, complex analysis, and statistics.

Music

There are two sections to the music test and three subscores. The subscores are in history and theory, listening and literature, and aural skills. In the first section of the test, you will be given approximately 50 multiple-choice questions and 15 questions that allow you to give your own response. The multiple-choice questions concern the theory and history of music from the Middle Ages to the present. The other questions ask about theory: cadences, key signatures, scales, clefs, harmonic analysis, chord-spelling, notation, and transposition.

The second section of the test will give you 61 multiple-choice questions and eight questions that allow you to give your own response. For these multiple-choice questions, you will hear a taped excerpt of music and will answer about five questions based on each excerpt (you will hear approximately twelve excerpts). The music may be from the Middle Ages to the present. The other questions are two harmonic dictations, one single-voice and one two-voice dictation, two part-writing exercises, and two counterpoint exercises.

Physics

You should be able to take this test based on taking three years of physics in college. There are about 100 questions, which are divided as follows: classical mechanics (20 percent); fundamentals of electromagnetism (18 percent); quantum mechanics (12 percent); thermodynamics and statistical mechanics (10 percent); atomic physics (10 percent); nuclear and particle physics, astrophysics, and condensed matter physics (9 percent); physical optics and wave phenomena (9 percent); laboratory methods (6 percent); and special relativity (6 percent).

Psychology

The psychology test has almost as many questions as the Literature in English test—218. You will get two subscores: one in experimental psychology and one in social psychology. Approximately 86 percent of the questions are divided between these two subjects. The remaining 14 percent of the questions will contribute to your overall score (which will also include the questions used for your two subscores). These questions are about measurement, research designs, statistics, applied psychology, and the history of psychology.

Sociology

The 185 questions in the sociology test cover 12 subfields that are normally included in a college sociology curriculum. Topics covered include urban/rural/community; inequality; social psychology; general theory; criminology and deviance; organizations; gender and family; intergroup relations (race, religion, and ethnicity); social change; social institutions; and demography.

Paper-Based Test vs. Computer-Based Test

Paper-Based	*Computer-Based*
Scores available in six weeks	Scores available instantly
Lasts 4 .5 hours	Lasts 4.5 hours
Costs $96.00	Costs $96.00
Offered only twice a year	Offered throughout the year
Can go back and change answers	Cannot change an answer
Same test is given to everyone	Test questions are tailored to your ability level

Now that you have some basic information about each of the standardized tests, you can turn to Chapter 11 and contact the testing agency for the test you need to take. Once you've contacted the testing agency, you can start thinking about when you actually want to take the test and how to best prepare for it. For most people, taking the standardized test is the first step down the road of the application process. The next chapter will help you take the next step of deciding which schools you should apply to.

Section 2

How to Get the Ball Rolling

Deciding Where To Apply

You may have known for a long time what type of graduate or professional degree you want to pursue, or you may have struggled (or still be struggling) trying to decide between graduate school, medical school, business school, or law school. If you thought that was a difficult decision, just wait until you start trying to decide what schools you should apply to. With almost 180 law schools, over 1,000 business schools, 125 medical schools, and hundreds of graduate schools, the choices can seem overwhelming. Some people take the easy way out and decide to apply only to the top-ranked schools in their discipline. This is foolish. While rankings may be a significant factor in your application decisions, they should not be the only factor. This chapter will show you the different characteristics you should think about as you are choosing potential schools.

Rina said that she was only going to apply to the top ten graduate programs in physics and if she wasn't admitted, she wasn't going to go to graduate school. She finally was convinced to send an application to one "non–top ten" school. She was admitted to one top ten school and to the "non–top ten" school. After careful consideration, she decided to attend the latter school because she realized it would suit her needs better. She ended up being very happy there and getting a great job after graduation.

Gathering Information

Chapter 9 will approach this topic from a different perspective and tell you what to take into account once you have actually been admitted and are in the enviable position of being able to choose among several offers. Too many applicants spend most of their time deciding among their offers rather than spending it deciding where to apply. The latter decision requires a great deal of your time and attention, since it will determine your later options. If you don't apply carefully now, you might find once you have been admitted that none of the schools are really right for you, and you may find yourself wishing that you had applied to other schools.

Alexandra had always wanted to attend medical school, because she knew she wanted to be a doctor. However, she didn't know much about medical school and what was involved. She talked to a few friends, a graduate of her school who was in medical school, and a professor. None of her conversations was very involved, and she didn't stop to think about what was important to her. Based on rather superficial reasons, she chose five schools. She was admitted to three of them, and then engaged in an extensive exploration of each of the schools. At that point, she realized that what she really wanted was to be a general practitioner in a small town, and all of the schools that had admitted her tended to train doctors who wanted to be very specialized and practice in big cities. Since none of the schools fit, she decided to wait for a year and spend that time investigating other schools and then only to apply to those where she thought she could be happy.

You will have to decide how much investigation of schools is enough before you apply. Most people will do some preliminary thinking about schools before they apply and will wait until they have been admitted to do an in-depth investigation of the schools and to visit them. This strategy is fine, as long as you make sure that your preliminary thinking takes into account your values and priorities and doesn't rely just on superficial considerations.

You can approach this decision-making process with a pyramid in mind. You will start out with a wide base that will include almost every school. At the base, you will be getting as much general information as you can about the type of graduate or professional school you are seeking. The next stage of the pyramid is to get information about specific schools. As you progress through the process and get more information, the pyramid will get smaller. Ultimately, of course, the pyramid will peak as you reach the top and you choose the one school you want to attend. For this chapter, though, the pyramid will stop somewhere in the middle range, where you have gotten past the base and have narrowed your choices down enough to know where you will be applying.

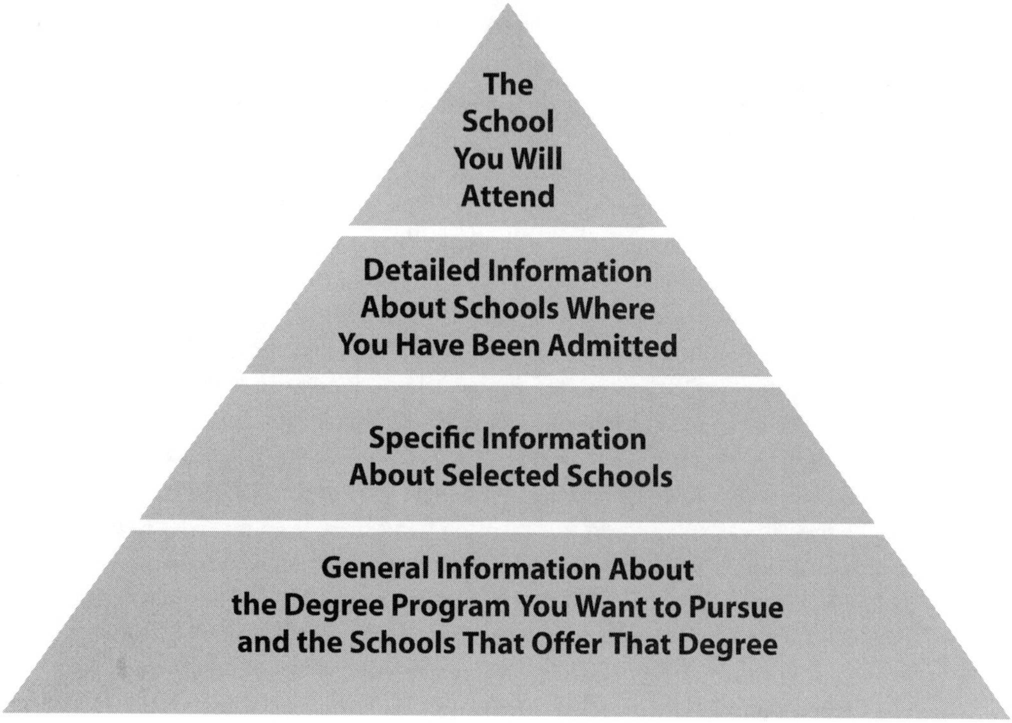

The School You Will Attend

Detailed Information About Schools Where You Have Been Admitted

Specific Information About Selected Schools

General Information About the Degree Program You Want to Pursue and the Schools That Offer That Degree

Getting General Information

When you are at the beginning stages of this process (the base of the pyramid), there are many sources of information you can use. Bookstores are full of books that specialize in the different graduate and professional schools. These books can give you general information about choosing schools but can also give you specific information about different schools.

You can also contact classmates who want to pursue the same type of degree as you. While they may be as lost as you are in the beginning, they may also know more than you. At the very least, you can support each other and point each other to sources of information you have found useful.

Recent graduates from your college who are currently enrolled in the program that interests you are even more valuable than classmates, because they have just gone through the process, so it is fresh in their minds. They can share with you what they learned when they were going through the admissions process, including what they found out about different schools and how they made their decisions of where to apply and where to attend.

If you don't know any graduates of your college who are attending the program that you want to pursue, you can contact your college's alumni office and see if they can put you in touch with anyone. If your college can't help you, try calling some of the graduate or professional school programs and asking if they can tell you whether anyone who is enrolled there graduated from your college.

Some graduate and professional schools may have an open house during the fall semester where prospective students are invited to come and learn more about the school. You will usually have a chance to interact with current students, faculty members, and administrators, and to take a tour of the school. Other activities could well be included during the day. You can find out if such a program is being offered at any school near you. Even if you don't think you are interested in that school, it's a great way to start finding out the types of information you need to know in order to evaluate schools.

You may have a wonderful resource very near you. If you are currently in school and your university has a graduate or professional school in the field which interests you or you are working and there is a university near you, you are fortunate. Even if you don't apply there, you have a good source of information quite close by. You can go to the school and ask questions of the students, the faculty, the admissions office, and the financial aid office. By getting an in-depth feel of one school, you can apply that knowledge to other schools and have a point of comparison for them.

Take advantage of the opportunity to get information from the graduate or professional school that is part of your university. It's an easy way to get valuable insight into the nature of graduate and professional school.

Your college may bring in alumni to speak to you about being a doctor, lawyer, business executive, or PhD. These speakers can again give you a wealth of information about graduate and professional schools generally. If you hear that someone is coming to campus who has the same degree that you want to get, go and talk to that speaker, even if the topic of their talk isn't of particular interest to you. You can ask the speaker questions afterward about graduate and professional school.

Start the process of information-gathering as early as possible. Don't wait until the last minute to begin exploring options.

It's a good idea to start building your base of knowledge about graduate and professional school as soon as you know you want to attend. Because information-gathering can take a long time, an early start is advisable.

Getting Information About Specific Schools

Your initial school research should have made you aware of a number of schools that might meet your needs. You then need to find out information about those specific schools. Start by contacting the schools and asking for their written materials. Try to be as specific as possible in your request, because schools often have a number of different publications and the admissions office won't always tell you what's available. That's not because they're trying to hide anything from you, but because they can't list every publication for every caller to see which ones they might like.

Schools may call the publication they send out a viewbook or a catalog or bulletin. Viewbooks are usually brochures with pictures that give you a general idea of the school but that don't provide lots of specific information. They generally don't contain course listings or give extensive biographies of faculty members. Catalogs and bulletins are usually very dense reading, often with small print and few pictures. They typically list in sometimes excruciating detail every fact you could want to know about a school, including course descriptions and full biographies of professors. Some schools may have a separate publication that specifically highlights their faculty. Others may have publications about specific specialties at that school. Still others might have separate financial aid publications or brochures written for certain subpopulations within the applicant pool (women and minorities are the most obvious, but some will have information for older applicants or applicants with children).

A school's Web site is often a better source of information than its printed materials. Because the Web can be updated easily and quickly (schools don't have to wait for annual publication deadlines), you may find more up-to-the-minute information on the Web. Although you don't want to be unduly swayed toward a school just because it has a beautiful Web site, the sophistication of the Web site can give you an idea of how technologically advanced a school is.

A school might have recent articles about itself that it could send you, or you could do a search of relevant newspapers or magazines to find articles. Since these articles are not written by the school, they may give you a more objective view than publications that are produced by the school.

An excellent source of information is the representatives sent out by the admissions offices. These representatives usually are admissions officers, but they may also be current students, alumni, or faculty members. They may come to your college specifically for an information session that has been set up at the college, or they may be attending a "Graduate and Professional School Forum" being held at your school. These forums are similar to the college fairs you might have attended when you were in high school. Each graduate or professional school will have a table with literature on it, and you will be able to walk up to the representatives to ask them questions about their schools. These forums may be general in nature and include many different types of graduate and professional schools, or they may be limited to one particular type of school, i.e., graduate business schools only.

Information forums are also held in cities across the country. GRE Forums on Graduate Education, MBA Forums, and Law School Forums are all held at hotels in major cities. Although these forums can be crowded and congested, a large number of schools attend them, so it is a convenient way to get information all in one place. It also allows you the opportunity to compare and contrast answers from different schools to the same question. After you have been at the forum and talked to a number of schools, you can go back to schools you saw at the beginning and ask them more in-depth, refined questions based on the new knowledge you have gained. The forums also typically offer seminars during the day on topics such as financial aid and the admissions process, so you can learn general information as well.

Calvin had been out of college for three years and was thinking about getting an MBA. He had gotten lots of general information about the programs and thought he was ready to pursue it, but he still wasn't convinced and didn't think he knew enough to be able to make the decision even to take the GMAT. Since he lived in a town where there was no university, he couldn't go there to find out more. When he found out that an MBA Forum was being held in a city a few hundred miles away, he bought a plane ticket and went. He was able to talk to many admissions representatives and to get enough information that he felt comfortable registering for the GMAT and pursuing admission to an MBA school.

When you first start the information-gathering process, you may be a sponge that is just soaking up as much information as you can get. You may not have much idea of what is important to you or whether one factor is more important than another. As you go through the process, you will find that the information you are collecting will start to inform your judgments, and you should be able to start forming ideas about what is most significant to you in terms of your goals and desires.

The following items are ones that you will probably want to consider at this stage of the process.

- Ranking
- Where you can get in
- How many schools should I apply to?
- Location
- Part-time versus full-time programs

- Joint degree programs
- Starting date
- Size
- Faculty
- Other students
- Cost
- Strengths or specialties
- Special programs
- Attending graduate school where you attended undergraduate school

Some of these factors—like size, faculty, cost, and strengths or specialties—are all covered in detail in Chapter 9, because generally they will matter the most to people at that point. You may be someone, though, for whom one or more of these factors is so important that it wouldn't be worth your considering a school that didn't meet your criteria. Thus, a brief discussion of these factors is considered here.

Ranking

We rank everything in our society, from sports teams to the richest people in the world. Even David Letterman has a top ten list on his show every night. It's no wonder then that rankings of graduate and professional schools are big business for publishers. It seems like everyone wants to know just how highly ranked a program is.

Rankings can be useful when they are understood and used in context and are not seen as the sole determinant of the quality of a school. Rankings can give you a general idea of a school's reputation. When you combine a ranking with the observations of others who are familiar with the school and its competitors and with your own observations, it can give you a benchmark by which to judge a school.

When you're using a particular ranking, you need to look at the methodology that was used to develop it. A ranking system reflects the values of those who designed the system, and those values might not be the same as yours. Some ranking systems might emphasize the starting salary of a program's graduates, while others will place more emphasis on the entering credentials of students in the program. Even if a ranking system takes into account the entering credentials, is more emphasis placed on test scores or undergraduate grade point averages? If one school has an entering class whose median GPA is 3.5 and median LSAT is 169, is that school better or worse than a school whose entering class has a median GPA of 3.8 and a median LSAT of 164? While a ranking system will devise some way to tell you which of those two schools is better, there might not be any real difference to you as a student attending that school.

Use ranking cautiously and judiciously in your evaluation.

While a general ranking may tell you something about how good a school is overall, it will not tell you anything about how good it is for individual specialties. A business school that has a high overall ranking might not be particularly good in finance. If you want to go into finance, you will care more about its strength in that area than you will in its overall strength. Some rankings now purport to rank specialties in addition to giving overall rankings, which can help with this situation. You can then look at the overall rank and the specialty rank and take both into consideration.

Rankings are most useful when you use two or more of them, because then you can use them to see if there is a consensus view of how the schools are perceived. Rankings should never be used to make fine distinctions among schools or to be the final arbiter of your decision of which school to attend, if two schools are ranked similarly. There is little real difference between a school that is ranked number 10 and a school that is ranked number 12.

It may be useful to go through some of the criteria that are employed in different rankings systems so you can be better educated as to how to view these rankings and can consider the relevance to you of the factors being included in the ranking. The following factors will be discussed:

- Reputation rank
- Resources
- Research activity
- Entering credentials
- Employment statistics

Reputation Rank

Most rankings include something that purports to measure reputation. Of course, some would argue that the school's overall rank is the measure of a school's reputation, but the rankers endeavor to capture this elusive reputation in a more precise way and have it actually count as part of the ranking. The most common way to determine a school's reputation is to survey people. Popular choices of those to be surveyed are academics and those who do the hiring in relevant fields.

When a dean or faculty member receives a survey asking her to rank her school and all other schools of the same type, she is most likely to rank highly the school that employs her and the school from which she graduated. There is a built-in incentive for her to do so.

In most cases, it takes a long time for the reputation of a school to change, even when the school itself has changed dramatically. A school that was once very strong with outstanding faculty may have suffered a number of faculty retirements, with no comparable people to replace them, yet in the minds of most people, the school will still be considered to be very good. Conversely, a school that has been weak can have a difficult time convincing the world that it is now a stronger institution.

A ranking system may also base its reputation section on a survey of those who tend to hire graduates of the programs being ranked.

Resources

A ranking system may include a component based on the resources available to the school. This could be calculated as the amount of money spent by the school divided by the total number of schools. This calculation may penalize a school that is able to run a lean, but outstanding, operation.

Research Activity

This component of a ranking system may take into account how much money a school receives for its research activities and/or the number of faculty members who engage in research. If research will be a major component of your graduate program, this aspect of a ranking system may be quite important to you. If research is not a major component, you might wish that faculty members would spend more time on their teaching than on their research.

Publishing is another component of a program's research activity. You might be very interested in knowing that faculty members have published extensively, because it shows that they are well regarded by others in the field. A strong publishing record can also show that faculty are on the "cutting edge" of their field.

This measurement factors in the undergraduate GPA and test scores for entering students. The ranking may use the medians for these two numbers or may use an average or some other figure. As with any statistics, these can be misleading. An applicant who has been out of school for 15 years and has had a very successful career but who had a 2.9 GPA while an undergraduate will be treated the same as someone who just graduated last year with a 2.9 GPA.

Employment Statistics

When employment statistics are used in a ranking system, the rank may factor in the number of employers who interviewed on campus divided by the number of students enrolled, the median starting salary of graduates, or the number of graduates who were employed within a certain period of time after graduation.

Flaws With the Ranking Systems

When considering rankings, keep in mind that the information used in the rankings is only as good as the people who provide it and those who interpret and publish it. In some ranking systems, schools' ranks can fluctuate by 20 or 30 places from one year to the next. Either the school has changed the way it has reported some important piece of information or the methodology of the ranking has changed during that year, because no school would have changed that much during one year.

In a recent year, a major ranking system announced shortly after it had published its rankings that it had discovered an error and that the rankings of a number of schools were actually different than what had been published. This caused great consternation among the affected schools, since the magazine had already been printed.

A ranking system typically will not take into account the quality of teaching at an institution, the nature of the student body, the location of the school, or any of a number of other factors that you will probably want to consider in your decision-making process. A ranking reflects only one perspective on what is most important in a school. You may not think the same factors are as important. As you are reading this book and going through the process of deciding on the right school for you, you will be getting the information you need to create your own ranking system. That ranking system should have the most weight when you are making your decisions about where to apply and where to attend.

Where You Can Get In

Of course, a critical factor when you're deciding where to apply is assessing your chances of being admitted. This is a very inexact art, as you will see in Chapter 5, but to the extent that you can figure out your admission chances at particular schools, you can use this vital fact to help you plot your admissions strategy.

If you go through all of the factors that are listed as to which schools would best suit you and then you find out that they only admit people in the top 5 percent of their undergraduate class and the top 2 percent of test-takers, it won't do you much good to apply only to them if you graduated in the top 20 percent of your undergraduate class and were in the top 10 percent of test-takers.

One way to find out your chances of admission is to look at school catalogs and see if they tell you anything about the type of students they admit. You will probably find very vague language about how they are looking for "the best and the brightest students who will add diversity to the classroom," but you may find some useful information, as well.

The school might include a list of schools where their current undergraduate students received their degrees. If you see that a large majority of the students attended a private, liberal-arts college in that region and you attended a public university across the country, it might be a clue that your chances of admission at that school aren't very good. Of course, if the school is truly seeking diversity, your application might be well received because the school doesn't have many students who fit your profile.

Another way to find out your probability of being admitted is to ask individual schools. Although predicting your exact chances of admission is impossible, it is possible to tell you whether you are in the range or not.

Isabel went to a Graduate School Forum being held at her college and asked the various graduate school representatives, "I have a 3.5 GPA in English from Penn State, and I got a 750 on the GRE General Test. Can you tell me if I will be competitive for admission at your school, or if it will be more of a long shot?" All of the representatives told her that the final admissions would depend on her complete application for admission, but based on what they heard about her GPA and test score, they could give her a very rough idea of her chances. One representative told her there was a good chance that she could be admitted to that school, another said that she was not very competitive at that school, and a third told her that it was impossible to tell her anything based on her numbers.

A third way to find out your chance of admission at a particular school is to see whether the school publishes any kind of admissions profile grid. For law schools, Law Services publishes a book that contains information about each of the accredited law schools. Most of the schools provide a grid for the book that shows LSAT scores across the top and GPAs down the side. Each box of the grid shows how many applicants with that range of LSATs and GPAs applied during the previous year and how many were admitted.

If you are interested in MBA programs, you can request a résumé book from the school. MBA programs publish these books with résumés of their current students to send to potential employers. Looking at these books will give you a good idea of the type of students who are enrolled, which in turn can give you a sense of the admissions criteria used by the school.

Most colleges or universities will have someone (either a professional staff person or a faculty member) who is designated as the pre-law adviser or the pre-med adviser for that school. Some of these advisers can be enormously helpful to you as you are trying to determine your chances for admission. If the advisers have been in the field for awhile and if your college sends many students on to law or medical schools, they will have seen how students from your college have fared in the admissions process at different law and business schools. They may even have statistics that will actually show you, in an anonymous way, past graduates and their credentials and where they were admitted.

Applicants considering graduate school can talk to their professors to find out similar information. Although the professors may not have as much detailed information as the pre-professional advisers, they still can tell you (usually from memory) which graduates were admitted where, how your record compares to theirs, and whether they think you have a good chance of being admitted to particular schools.

If you use these techniques to assess your chances of admission, you can then devise an admissions strategy that takes this into account and maximizes your chance of admission. For this approach to work, you must be honest with yourself about the strengths and liabilities of your application and you must look at your application from the point of view of an admissions officer, who sees hundreds or thousands of applications every year. If you think you are being too unrealistic in your choice of schools, ask someone objective (not your parents) for advice, and listen to it.

Marc decided that he wanted to go to a "top" law school and proceeded to apply to only six schools, all of which were highly unlikely to admit him. He spoke with his pre-law adviser (who had been in the business for over 20 years), who told him that he would almost certainly be rejected from all of those schools but that there were other schools that were very good and that would probably admit him. Mark chose to stick to his original plan and applied only to the six schools he had identified. Although he knew that his GPA and LSAT were not competitive for those schools, he felt that he had experience that couldn't be matched by any other applicant and that the schools would place more weight on his experience than on his numbers. The fact was that his experience wasn't so unique and so couldn't compensate for his less-than-stellar college performance and LSAT score. He was rejected by all six schools and was left wondering why.

Generally, you should divide schools into four categories: unattainable without a miracle, reach schools, middle schools, and safety schools.

Unattainable Schools

Unattainable schools are those where your chance of admission is so slim that there is no point in you wasting your time and money in applying there. An obvious example would be an MBA program that requires three years of work experience and you only have one year. Some of you may be such strong candidates that you will think that no school is unattainable. That's fine, if it's true. Don't be so blinded by your own greatness, though, that you fail to see when you are trying to achieve the impossible.

Reach Schools

Reach schools are schools where you have a chance of being admitted, but the admissions committee will have to stretch a bit in order to do so. Every applicant should apply to at least one reach school. If you don't, you may find that you have shortchanged yourself and relegated yourself to attending a lower-quality school when you could have attended a higher-quality one. The difference between a reach school and an unattainable school can often be slight, so again, you have to try to be honest with yourself during the process.

Kelly approached me at a professional school fair and said that she had always wanted to attend my school. She didn't think she had a chance, though. I told her that if her heart was really set on it, she might want to apply just so she would know that she had tried. As we talked further and she told me more about the strength of her application, I told her that it was highly unlikely that she would be admitted and suggested that unless she had the $75 application fee to spare and she wanted to spend time completing the application, she would probably be wasting her time applying. Elizabeth approached me at the same fair and asked a similar question. Since her credentials were slightly stronger, I told her that she stood a *slim* chance of being admitted but emphasized that it was a slim chance. She decided to apply to my school as a "reach" school. She put together such a great application that she was admitted.

You have to decide when your dream school is realistic enough that it is worth putting it in the reach school category and applying and when it is so unrealistic that it should be placed in the unattainable category.

Middle Schools

These are the schools where it is very hard to predict your chances of admission because you are so similar to others who are already there. If you are an "average" applicant for that school based on your background, GPA, and test score, your chances of being admitted are probably about 50–50, which would make this a middle school. The majority of your applications should be to schools that fall into this middle category.

Safety Schools

Safety schools are those where you know you stand a very good chance of being admitted. If you are serious about attending school, you should apply to at least one safety school. This will ensure that even if all other schools turn you down, you will still have one option open to you.

How Many Schools Should I Apply To?

There is no magic number of schools to which you should apply. The numbers vary from the extreme of one school to the opposite extreme of 50 schools. You may find that there are only three schools that really meet your needs. If you have done careful research and are certain of your conclusions, three is the right answer for you. Conversely, you may find 20 schools that you think would be a good match for you. That number is probably too high, and you will want to do some more research to narrow down your choices.

If you are a particularly strong candidate, you may not need to apply to many schools, because your chances of admission will be good everywhere. If you are a particularly weak candidate, you may need to apply to a large number of schools in order to find one where you will be admitted.

> Generally, people will apply to somewhere between five and ten schools. Because medical school admissions is currently so competitive, some applicants will apply to 20 or more schools to increase their chances of being admitted. The average number of applications for medical school is nine to ten.

The decision of how many schools to apply to depends on your budget, as much as anything else. Application fees can range from $50–$150 per school, so you need to be realistic about how many applications you can afford. If interviews are part of the process, you will also have to figure in the cost of flying out for those. Don't be so frugal that you only apply to three or four schools for financial reasons. This is part of the investment in your future, and if you have to scrimp and save in order to apply to a reasonable number of schools, you should probably do so.

> Many schools offer application fee waivers for applicants who are truly needy. In evaluating your application for a fee waiver, they will generally take into account both your parents' financial situation and your own financial situation.

You will also want to think about how much time you want to devote to the process of applications. If you are applying to programs where the applications are relatively similar, you will find that it isn't so much harder to complete four applications as it is to complete one, since once you have put in the work needed for one of them, the rest will be easy. If the applications for the programs to which you're applying are so different from each other that each one is an odyssey unto itself, you may want to give serious consideration to how many you want to complete.

Location

For some of you, location may be your primary consideration. Location will probably be important to all of you at some point in your decision-making process, but some people are so mobile that they could go to school in any part of the country and will only start to consider location once they have been admitted. Chapter 9 goes into great detail about numerous considerations to take into account with respect to location.

If you are not mobile, you will have to consider location as paramount in your deliberations from the very beginning. This would be true if you were working and wanted to keep your job and go to school part-time or if you were married and your spouse had a good job and was unwilling to relocate or any other reason that would make you want to attend school in a very definite location.

What should you do if you don't feel geographically mobile but you can't find a school in the area that meets your needs? If you're working for a large company, you could find out if there are branches in other parts of the country and whether a transfer would be feasible.

You could see if it would be feasible to do your job while telecommuting from another location. With the remarkable advances that have been made in technology, it can be possible to do some jobs from anywhere in the country, as long as you have access to a computer modem, a fax, and express mail services. An admissions director for a California school actually did her job while living in Hawaii. She could do recruiting travel from any airport in the country, she could keep in touch via e-mail and faxes, and she could have application files sent to her by express mail.

If you're intending to pursue a one- or two-year program and you plan to work for the same company after getting your graduate degree, you could ask your employer for a leave of absence, relocate somewhere else for school, and then return to your original location after graduation.

If you're married and your spouse doesn't want to relocate because of his or her wonderful job, you could consider being apart for the length of your schooling. Some students find this works well, because it frees them from distractions while they are in school and makes them more efficient at studying, so that when they are able to spend a weekend with their spouse, they can focus on each other.

Randi wanted to attend graduate school in Philadelphia, but she and her family lived in Pittsburgh. Her husband had a great job, the children enjoyed their school, and they wanted to live in Pittsburgh after she graduated. They decided that Randi would go to school in Philadelphia, while the family stayed in Pittsburgh. She went home about one weekend a month, and the family came to see her about one weekend a month. Although it was a struggle, it was the best resolution they could find that met everyone's needs.

Most often people think of location in terms of urban versus rural locations. Unless you know yourself well enough to know that you would be absolutely miserable living in an urban location, you probably shouldn't limit your search to rural locations, and vice versa. Many people make unwarranted assumptions about a location without ever having seen it, and it may be that the perfect school for you may not be in the most desirable location for you, but you may be able to live with it, given all of the other excellent attributes of the school. The point here is not to be too narrow-minded about location, unless you have a very clear and specific reason for doing so.

Ideally, you would visit every school before you ever applied so that you would have a very good sense of the nature of the place, but that is not realistic for most people, since they have neither the time nor the money to make that kind of trip. If you can't visit, the school's written materials can often give you a fair idea of the surrounding area, enough for you to form an impression of whether you would be happy there.

Part-time Versus Full-time Programs

One of your initial decisions should be whether you want to attend school part-time or full-time. If you want to attend part-time, you will find that your choice of schools is immediately more limited. While all schools that offer part-time programs also offer full-time programs, the reverse is not true. Some schools will only offer full-time programs, so you can strike them off your list if you are certain you don't want to go to school full-time.

Joint Degree Programs

Perhaps you have decided that you want to pursue two graduate or professional degrees at the same time (some might call you a masochist). Many joint degree programs are available at different schools. Particularly popular are JD/MBA programs for those who want to be an entrepreneur or MD/PhD programs for those who want to pursue scientific research. The advantage of a joint degree program is that each degree program agrees to accept credits from the other program toward its degree, so you are able to get both degrees in a shorter amount of time than would be required if you pursued the degrees independently. For example, it would take five years to get a law degree and a master's degree in business if you did them separately. However, if you were accepted into a joint JD/MBA program, you could get both degrees in only four years.

Joint degrees are not for everyone and are not to be taken lightly. While the time commitment and cost are less than they would be if you got both degrees independently, they are more than getting only one degree. You shouldn't pursue a joint degree just because you aren't sure which of two degrees you want to earn. Deciding to get them both at the same time just postpones the inevitable decision of which field you ultimately want to pursue. The happiest and most successful joint degree students are those who have a clear idea of what they want to do and how it will call upon the knowledge and skills they will get from earning both degrees.

Getting a joint degree is *not* the same as getting a double major in college. While many students are able to get two majors in the same amount of time it would take them to get one major, it always requires additional time to get two degrees.

If you decide that you want to get a joint degree, you clearly must factor that in when you are deciding where to apply. Not all schools offer joint degrees, and not all that offer them make them easy to pursue. If a school doesn't offer a joint degree program, you can easily strike it from your list.

You may decide to strike a school from your list if the admissions process for the joint degree program is too burdensome. Some schools require you to take two standardized tests (one for each of the programs) and to go through the entire application process for each of the two programs. Others will have a more integrated approach to the admissions process and will allow you to fill out only one application and to take only one standardized test.

If you find that one of the degree programs at a school is much weaker than the other degree program you want to pursue, you may decide that you don't want to apply to that school.

Starting Date

All schools have an entering class that starts sometime in the fall, usually between August and October. Schools might offer additional options and allow you to start in winter (usually January) or the summer (usually May to June). These alternative starting dates may be of interest to you if you are graduating from college in the middle of the year and wish to enter graduate or professional school right away rather than taking some time off. If you are older and working, you may be anxious to start right away and don't want to wait until the fall.

Since you will seriously limit your options if you decide to consider only schools that offer starting times in addition to the traditional fall start, you should think carefully about how important it is to you that you start at a time other than the fall.

This may seem obvious, but you should also calculate how much time there will be between your college graduation and the start of your post-baccalaureate studies. If you can't graduate until August and have to start school in the fall, you should make sure that you will actually be finished with your college classes before your other school starts.

Brian applied for a joint degree program that started in June. He was admitted in January and sent the information about when classes would start. In late May, he suddenly realized that his college graduation was not going to take place until two days after he was supposed to start graduate school. For some reason, it had never occurred to him to check the dates and make sure that they were in sync. He was able to start in the program, but he missed going through his graduation ceremony.

Size

Many applicants will not have a definite enough idea of the size of school they want to attend to consider ruling out a school based only on its size. But if this is a major concern for you, you should apply only to those schools that meet your size requirement. If you think you will only thrive in a small school, then you should only apply to small schools. You may want to keep an open mind here, though, and find out more details about the size of the school. If the entering class is large but the courses are small, the environment may be similar enough to a small school that you will be happy there.

Faculty

The quality of the faculty and your interactions with them can make or break your experience in graduate school. Read Chapter 9 carefully about the characteristics you should be looking for in faculty and see if there are any schools you can weed out at the preapplication stage based on the faculty.

Faculty are also important for professional school students, but at this point, you may just want to assure yourself that the faculty is well qualified and highly regarded and leave the searching questions regarding the faculty to after you have been admitted.

Other Students

As you are determining your chances of admission at a school, you will learn a lot about the quality of students (at least as measured by numbers) who are currently enrolled there. You will also learn something about the quality of undergraduate institutions they attended and may get some idea of how accomplished they are outside of the classroom. These students will be your peers throughout school and your professional career, so you want to find out if they are the type of people with whom you want to associate.

While you probably wouldn't be considering graduate or professional school unless you were quite accomplished and competitive, you might decide that in your post-college work, you don't want to be the most accomplished person in the classroom. You may wish that you were more in the middle of the class so that you could learn from others and not always have to be the teacher of others.

Leslie had been a high achiever throughout her life. She got straight As all the way through high school and only got a few Bs in college. She wasn't necessarily the brightest student, but she was smart and she worked very hard. She was admitted to graduate programs, where, based on the profile of the other students, she could have continued to be at the top of her class, but she decided that she wanted to go to a school where she would really be challenged, even if that meant being in the middle of the class or worse. She decided to take the chance of being the proverbial small fish in a big pond rather than taking the route that would more likely have assured her of being the big fish in a small pond.

Cost

Your financial situation may be such that you think you should limit your choices only to low-cost schools. While this might be the right decision for you, don't forget to consider the possibility of financial aid (see Chapter 8). Especially if you are attending a PhD program, there is a strong likelihood that you will be offered full funding from at least one of the schools that admits you. Even attending professional school, you may be offered a scholarship from an expensive private school that will make the cost cheaper than going to a less expensive public school.

Don't decide not to apply to a school based on its cost alone, unless you know that you can't get any financial aid there and you can't afford it without financial aid. Your ultimate decision of whether to attend a school based on cost should come after you have received your financial aid offer.

As you're getting specific information, you may find out that a school offers only need-based scholarships and will take into account your parents' financial situation (remember that this is an individual school's decision and that you are always considered independent of your parents for the purposes of federal loans). Perhaps you won't qualify for a scholarship from that school because your parents have too much money. You may decide not to apply to that school if your parents won't support you and you aren't willing to borrow to finance the entire cost of your education.

You may want to keep cost in mind as you are deciding on the mix of schools to which you will apply and make sure that you have some lower-cost schools on your list, in case finances do become a major concern once you have been admitted. A school may cost less because it charges less tuition or because it is located in a part of the country where you can live rent-free (with parents or other relatives, for example). Public schools are also cheaper than private schools if you are a resident of the state where the school is located.

Strengths or Specialties

You may want to consider whether a school has particular strengths or specialties and whether those match your interests. For some types of programs, this type of consideration will be more important than for other programs. It also will be more or less important to you depending upon how certain you are of your preferences. If you want to get a PhD in Elizabethan literature, minus other compelling reasons, it probably doesn't make sense for you to attend a school where the faculty's primary interests are in 20th century literature.

Special Programs

It may be that you are interested in some type of special program that is only offered at certain schools. An example of this would be an executive MBA program (where you attend school on the weekends). If you know you want a special program you should limit your search to only those schools that offer that type of program.

Attending Graduate School Where You Received Your Undergraduate Degree

If you are interested in graduate school you should ask your major department whether the school discourages you from applying for a master's or a doctorate from that school. If the department is small, there may not be enough courses offered to satisfy both advanced undergraduate students and beginning graduate students. Therefore, the school may suggest that you pursue your graduate degree elsewhere.

You have done a great job of taking the time to decide what is most important to you in a school and then considering different schools in light of those characteristics. At this stage, you are ready to start applying. Chapter 5 will take you through the admissions process from start to finish and will give you all of the necessary tools to make your application as strong as possible.

chapter 5

The Admissions Process

Now that you have gone through a self-assessment process, positioned yourself for admission, taken a standardized test, and decided where to apply, you want to know how to apply in order to maximize your chances of admission. This chapter will tell you exactly how to do that. You will learn how the admissions process really works and will find out about the various components of an application, including the application itself (including electronic applications), letters of recommendation, personal statements or essays, interviews, your transcript, and your standardized test scores. The chapter will also cover timelines for applying, early action options, and misconduct in the admissions process. We'll start with the components of an application.

Application

The first step in applying to every program except medical school (that topic is covered a bit later in this chapter) is to get an application from every school to which you want to apply. This is not as easy as it sounds, especially if you are applying to graduate school. The reason for this is that the graduate school may have one generic application, but individual departments may have their own applications that you have to complete instead of or in addition to the generic application.

If you're applying to graduate school, it's best to call the department first to find out if that department has its own application or if you have to complete the Graduate School application. You can also find out whether the department has its own printed material about the program and you can request that at the same time. Even if the department has its own literature, it's best to get a copy of the Graduate School Bulletin, because it will have general information about the university and about graduate school rules and policies that will apply to you.

If you're applying to law or business school, getting application materials is much easier. You only need to deal with the school to which you're applying and you don't have to contact the university. You can request materials by telephone, e-mail, or, in some cases, by the school's Web site.

Be patient if the materials don't arrive the week after you request them. Many schools send the materials bulk rate rather than first class, so it may take a few weeks to get them in the mail. If you haven't received anything about three to four weeks after you have requested materials, you may want to call the school to find out if your request was received and processed. Because many schools have high volumes of requests for applications, it is not uncommon for some to be misplaced, either in the office, or in the mail, so it pays to check (but not to be a pest!).

Joe sent in a request for an application using the school's Web site. The next day he sent an e-mail to the admissions office asking for an application. The following day he used the Web site again. The next day he called and requested an application. Since the school tracks all of its requests, the admissions office knew that he had asked for materials a number of times without waiting to see if they had been sent. By keeping your requests reasonable, you make less work for the admissions office and make it more likely that they will be able to fulfill your first request in a timely manner.

Once you have received the applications, read them carefully to find out the exact requirements of each school. While this chapter will cover the common aspects of applications, there can be differences from school to school, such as one school requiring two letters of recommendation and one school requiring three. Thus, it is crucial that you make sure that you have read each school's instructions and done exactly what that school requires of you.

Don't assume that an application for one type of graduate or professional program is the same as the application for that same type of program at another school.

You'll find that some application forms are quite simple and will ask only for basic background information. The schools then ask you to submit additional information as attachments to the application form. Other schools have lengthy applications and will ask for detailed information on the application form itself. They may give you the option of attaching that information on a separate sheet, or they may ask you to include everything on the application itself. Be certain to read the directions, so you know exactly what each school is asking or requiring.

Many applicants worry that if they don't have a typewriter to complete their application forms (not many people even have access to typewriters in this computer age), they will be disadvantaged. Unless the application specifically says that it has to be typed, you do not have to worry that you will have any problem if you neatly hand-write the application form (*neatly* is the operative word here). If people can't read your application, especially the information that has to be entered into the computer, like your name and address, you may have a problem in the admissions process.

While it is okay to hand-write your application form, you should use a word processor for any addendum or other piece of paper that is submitted with your application form.

Some schools have resolved the problem of lack of access to typewriters by making electronic applications available. That topic is covered in the following section.

Electronic Applications

Some schools offer an electronic application through their Web sites. You may be able to complete the application online and then submit it electronically, or you may be able to download the application, complete it, and then mail it in. With the latter method, you will still be faced with the issue of not having a typewriter, but at least you can download the application and have it available instantly without having to wait for the school to mail it to you.

Schools also might offer their application on a floppy disk that will be sent to you when you request an application. You complete the application on the disk and then send the disk to the school. The school can download the information from the disk into their database and not have to retype the information you have provided.

Another possibility for filling out your applications is to purchase a CD-ROM or floppy disk that contains a number of applications from different schools. These products are currently available for business school and law school (see Chapter 11 for information). One advantage of these products is that you select the schools to which you want to apply and then you have to answer common questions (like your name, address, and undergraduate school) only once. The software puts those answers into the appropriate places on each application you are completing. The software then asks you to answer any questions that are specific to each school to which you are applying and it formats those answers into the appropriate places on the applications. Another advantage to these programs is that you can edit and fine-tune your answers until you are sure you have written exactly what you want. You then print out the applications, proofread them carefully, and send them off to the schools.

Schools are happy to receive applications created from commercially available software. The schools have worked with the software providers to ensure that the applications meet their specifications, so you will not be disadvantaged if you use one of these software programs.

If you use a software program to complete your applications, you should still get an application from each school, because these applications will contain complete instructions, which may not be included in the software program. The application packets you get from the schools will also will contain any additional forms you may need to complete your application (the software will only have the application itself).

Medical schools have perfected the art of simplifying the application process. You can apply to most medical schools in the United States by completing only one application. This topic is covered in the following section.

Medical School Applications

The vast majority of medical schools (110 out of 125 schools in the United States) participate in a service called the American Medical College Application Service (AMCAS). AMCAS is a centralized service to which applicants submit just one application that is then sent to all schools designated by the applicant. AMCAS is available as a paper application or can be downloaded from the Web (**http://www.aamc.org/stuapps/admiss/amcas/start.htm**), completed on your computer, and mailed in on a computer disk. The application fee for AMCAS is $50.00 for the first school with an additional charge for each extra school.

Another application system that your medical school may use is the University of Texas System Medical and Dental Application Center (UTSMDAC). If you are applying to medical schools in Ontario, Canada, you will need to apply through the Ontario Medical School Application Service (OMSAS). Both of these services are similar to AMCAS. Contact information about them is contained in Chapter 11.

Letters of Recommendation

Letters of recommendation are an interesting part of the admissions process. Many admissions officers who are willing to be candid will tell you that they are not necessarily a crucial part of the admissions process (of course this varies from school to school), yet most schools require, or at least will accept, letters of recommendation. This section will try to shed some light on this apparent contradiction.

Letters of recommendation have become less helpful in the admissions process because they are nearly always glowing and full of praise for the "best student I have taught in the last 10 years." It can be hard to distinguish among such positive recommendations, especially if the person reading the recommendation is not personally acquainted with the recommender and has no context within which to place the recommendation.

Yet letters sometimes can make a real difference in an application, even making an admissions committee look more closely at an application it otherwise might have rejected. When can they make this difference? A recommendation can make a difference when it is written by someone who clearly knows you and your intellectual capacity well. It can also make a difference if the people on the admissions committee have read other recommendations from the recommender in the past and so have some basis for comparison and judgment.

Recommendations can also make a difference when all of the recommendations are uniformly strong and consistent with each other. If one recommendation says that you are quiet and the other says that you talk all the time in class, the likelihood is that the admissions committee will discount both recommendation letters because it won't know which one to believe.

Recommendation letters can also affect your application in a negative way. A bad letter (luckily they are few and far between) will almost certainly cause an admissions committee to reject you or at least to seek additional information about you. Even an apparently positive recommendation may not help you if it is written in such a way that it implies the writer is saying something else. "Ann is a solid student" may mean that Ann is great and "solid" is a positive adjective for the writer, or it may mean that Ann is someone who works hard and isn't particularly brilliant. Admissions committees have had lots of experience at reading between the lines of recommendations, so they often know what the recommender is trying to say.

One recommender has a system where he uses underlines and exclamation points to show what he really thinks about applicants. Admissions committees that get a lot of letters from this recommender know that the more exclamation points and underlines he uses at the end of the letter, the more highly he regards the applicant.

Since there is no way for you to know in advance with any certainty how important letters of recommendation are to a particular school, it is best for you to proceed on the assumption that they will make a difference in your application and plan accordingly. You might think that you have little control over your letters of recommendation, but in fact, you have a great deal of control, starting with choosing who should write letters for you.

Selecting People to Write Your Letters of Recommendation

Choosing who should write your letters of recommendation is a very important part of the application process, because your choices will determine what kind of letters will be written on your behalf.

Schools will tell you if they are looking for a particular type of person to write your letters of recommendation. In most cases, if you are coming right out of college or have been out only a short period of time, schools will prefer that your letters come from professors who have taught you as an undergraduate and who can speak to your intellectual ability.

If you have done honors work or an independent study, the professor who supervised your work (assuming you did a good job) is a good person to ask for a recommendation.

If you have been out of school for a period of time, it may be better for you to get letters of recommendation from a work supervisor rather than from a professor. In fact, some MBA programs may prefer letters from those who have worked with you, because they may think that people who have worked with you in a business setting will be able to speak more cogently of your ability to succeed in the business world than a professor will.

What is most important in choosing recommenders is to find out what each school requires or suggests. If a school has a requirement for getting a letter from a particular kind of person (for example, a professor), and you don't know any professors well enough for them to write for you, you should call the school and ask for alternative suggestions. If the school simply *suggests* that a letter should be from a professor and you don't know a professor well enough, then you don't need to call the school; you can select someone else who is appropriate.

Let's assume that you are in a situation where you could ask a number of people to write letters of recommendation for you. How should you choose among them? First, think about who knows you the best. You want recommenders who can speak clearly and eloquently about your abilities, and the best way for them to do that is to know you well. Just because you got an "A" in a class doesn't necessarily mean that the professor knows you. You might have never spoken up in class, or the class might have been too large for the professor to know you. You will know whether the professor knows you or will just look at the grade book to see what grade you earned in a course.

A school received a letter of recommendation that said, "Pravin received an 'A' in my course in Organic Chemistry. It was a very difficult course, and I am known as a tough grader." That letter did not tell the admissions committee much more than it could find out from the transcript. You want your letters of recommendation to add to your application, not just to duplicate information that can be found elsewhere.

Some applicants make the mistake of thinking that if someone is famous or is well known in the field they want to enter, that person is a good one to write a letter for them. They are wrong. A recommendation from a famous person who doesn't know you well and who can only say that "Peter seems nice and was eager when I met him" aren't very helpful to your quest of gaining admission.

Sarah was applying to law school and she asked a family friend, who happened to be a judge, to write a letter of recommendation for her. His letter was two pages long and went on at great length about how he had known Sarah's family for years and how they were all well accomplished professionals. He recounted the achievements of her grandparents, parents, aunts, and uncles, yet he said very little about Sarah herself. It was clear that he knew her simply as a family friend, but he didn't know anything about her analytical abilities or her suitability for a legal career.

This may seem odd, but you should try to find recommenders who like you. Knowing you well usually goes hand in hand with liking you, so this shouldn't be too hard. If the recommenders like you, they may well work harder on your letter of recommendation, and their respect and admiration for you will come through in the letter.

To the extent that you can ascertain this, you should find recommenders who are good writers. A well-written letter of recommendation is far more compelling than a poorly written letter that contains grammatical mistakes and typographical errors, even if both letters say exactly the same thing about you.

A recommendation letter that says, "Yvonne's writing skill are excellent," is not going to make much of an impression. The admissions committee will wonder whether the writer left off the "s" on the "skill," making it a typographical error, or whether the writer doesn't know that "skills" should be used in this sentence rather than "skill."

Try to find people who are reliable and who will follow through on their commitments to write letters for you. If someone knows you well and likes you, that person is more likely to be reliable, but if the person has been unreliable in the past when you have needed something or when the person has promised something, that should be a warning sign to you to be careful about whether the person will perform this task reliably.

When you ask someone to write a letter of recommendation for you, recognize that it will be a serious commitment of time on that person's part and don't go into the process assuming that the person will automatically say yes or that you have a right to get a letter from that person. Don't ask someone for a letter "on the fly." Make an appointment and sit down with the person and tell him or her exactly what you hope to do and why you would like a letter of recommendation from him or her.

Don't hesitate to ask the person whether he or she can write a "good" letter of recommendation for you. This gives the person a gracious way of declining your request without having to say that he or she would rather not write a letter for you. If someone you have asked to write a letter says no for any reason, accept that answer. Don't think that if you just break down his her barriers, it will be all right. You are likely to end up with a quickly written, uninformative letter. Worse yet, the person could procrastinate to the point where the letter reaches the school after the deadline.

Edward came and asked me to write a letter of recommendation for him. Since I had never had him in a class and he was applying for a graduate program, I suggested that he should ask one of his professors. He said that he didn't know any of them well enough. I asked if there were other people who knew him. I kept trying to give him reasons why he should get someone else to write the letter, but he ignored my hints. Since I was reluctant to tell him straight out that I would prefer not to write the letter, I ended up writing it. The letter was not very useful, because I had little specific I could say about his intellectual abilities. I could only talk about his personality and his character. While those are important characteristics, admissions committees want recommendations that speak to intellectual ability.

Once your recommender has agreed to write a letter of recommendation for you, you will want to make the process as easy as possible for the recommender. The next section covers that topic.

Information to Provide to a Recommender

You should give each recommender as complete and organized a packet of information as possible. This should include a list of schools to which you are applying and their deadline dates. You should also include stamped, addressed envelopes. Since the recommender is doing you a large favor, you want to make the process as easy as possible for him or her.

Whether a recommender gives a letter of recommendation back to you to be mailed with your application or sends the recommendation letter directly to the school, most schools prefer that the recommender sign the sealed flap of the envelope containing the letter to show that you have not seen it. If this is a school's requirement, share it with the recommender.

If schools have their own forms that the recommender must complete, include those forms in the packet you give the recommender. Be sure that you have filled in the biographical data on these forms like your name and

Social Security number. If a school provides a form but says that the recommender can simply sign the form and attach it to a letter written on letterhead, let the recommender know that that option exists.

If different schools want a recommender to cover different subjects in a letter of recommendation, make each school's requirements clear to the recommender. Don't expect the recommender to have to read through all of the forms to figure out what's required or what's most important.

Highlight the most important pieces of information on each recommendation form or summarize the information on a sheet of paper that includes all school's requirements. This will make it easy for the recommender to see at a glance what is required for each school.

Some applicants will provide the recommender with a copy of their personal statement or essay, their transcript, and their résumé. These latter pieces of information can give the recommender a more complete picture of you.

If you have a particular weakness in your application that you think a recommender can address, let the recommender know about that weak spot and why you think that weakness should be overlooked. Weak spots might include a low standardized test score, a poor semester of grades, or low grades in your first two years when you were taking courses in a major that you later changed. The recommender might be able to include some of that information in the letter. Don't assume, however, that a recommender can make up for an entire application that is weak.

Some schools will provide you with a form to sign that indicates that you have waived your right of access to that letter. The common wisdom is that it is best to waive your right of access because it will help the writer be more willing to write a candid letter, and the admissions committee will take the letter more seriously. If you have followed the steps outlined in this chapter of selecting your recommenders carefully, asking for a good letter of recommendation, and providing appropriate information to the recommender, you shouldn't have to worry about ever seeing the letter. You can feel confident that the recommender will write you as good a letter as possible.

Once the recommender has written a letter for you, remember that person and keep him or her apprised of your progress during the admissions process. When you are admitted to schools, you should acknowledge the recommender's role in your admission and thank that person.

Deadlines

Most schools will give you an application deadline, but recommend that you submit your application as early as possible. If a school's application deadline isn't until March and you want to submit your application in December, it is perfectly acceptable to tell your recommenders that your deadline is December. You are in control of the process and should be able to submit your application at the time you think will be most advantageous for you.

You can help your recommenders by asking them to write your letters as far in advance of the deadline as possible. Recognize, however, that they won't necessarily start working on the letters right away. They may see the extended deadline as an opportunity not to have to write the letter until sometime in the future. You can help your recommenders by calling them about a month before the deadline and asking them how the letter is coming along and whether they need any additional information you can provide. If you get the impression at that point that one of your recommenders won't get the letter done by the deadline, you can ask somebody else to write one.

Number of Recommendations to Submit

Schools will require anywhere from zero to four letters of recommendation to complete your application. You may occasionally wish to submit more letters than are required, but you should do so carefully. Think about whether the letters will add something valuable to your application or whether you are just feeling nervous and would like to have an extra feeling of security. Schools receive hundreds or thousands of applications every year, so they know what they are looking for. They have chosen their requirements carefully and are confident that they can select students based on the number of letters of recommendation that they require.

If, after thinking through your own situation, you decide that you wish to submit additional letters of recommendation, you should only submit one to two letters more than are required. Do not inundate an admissions committee with six, seven, or eight letters that have not been requested. The committee will end up questioning your judgment rather than reading your letters.

One applicant decided that more letters were better, perhaps on the theory that quantity mattered more than quality. He printed up postcards that said, "John Doe should be admitted to X School's Graduate Program, because he is a fine fellow." He distributed these postcards at the local mall and got people to sign them so he could send them in. These "recommendations" were obviously meaningless, and he was not admitted.

Perhaps the best case for sending an additional letter of recommendation is if a school only requires two letters and states a preference for those letters to be from professors. You have two professors who can write excellent letters for you, but you also have been working for a few years in a field related to that which you want to study, and your supervisor can write a strong letter about your abilities. In that case, adding a third letter will give the admissions committee a different perspective on you and your abilities, and the third letter could well add something to the committee's understanding of your suitability for the program you wish to enter.

Letter Services Through Schools

Some colleges and universities provide a centralized letter of recommendation service. This service may be provided through a pre-law adviser's office, a premedical adviser's office, or a career services office. Even if you have graduated, you can generally take advantage of this service at your alma mater.

A centralized letter of recommendation service allows your recommenders to write only one letter and to send it to the appropriate office at the university. That office then copies all of the letters and sends them to the graduate and professional schools in one packet. This can save both you and your recommender some time and is a clear advantage to both of you.

If one of your recommenders graduated from a program to which you are applying, you might ask that recommender not to use the centralized service for that school but to send a letter directly to the school in question. This will allow the recommender to tailor the letter and perhaps make more of an impact.

Check with your undergraduate school to find out if it offers a centralized letter of recommendation service that you can use.

Many graduate and professional schools will accept letters from these centralized services, or else the universities wouldn't offer them. If you use the service, you will not need to give the recommender any of the forms from the schools, since those forms will not be included in your overall packet. If you find a form that you think asks particularly good questions that you would like the recommender to consider when writing your letter, you should give that form to the recommender and explain why you are providing it.

If you use a centralized service, be certain to give the office providing the service a list of schools to which you will be applying. Also include the schools' addresses and deadline dates. Follow up with the office after you know all of your recommendation letters have been submitted to find out whether the letters have actually been mailed to the schools.

Medical School Recommendations

Many colleges and universities will have a pre-medical committee that will write your letters of recommendation for you. This committee may be called the Health Professions Advisory Committee. If your school has such a committee, you will want to find out what information the committee needs and whether the committee requires or recommends an interview as part of the process.

Dean's Certification

Some schools may require you to submit a *dean's certification.* This is a form provided by the school that you ask a dean or other appropriate official at your college to complete. The primary purpose of a dean's certification is to determine whether you have been the subject of any disciplinary actions while you were in school. The form might also ask about the rigor of your course load, your class rank, how many of your courses included a substantial writing component, or whether your SAT or ACT score accurately predicted your performance in college.

Although the form may ask other questions that présumé some personal knowledge of the applicant, the schools stress that they don't expect the person completing the form to know the applicant personally and that those questions do not have to be answered if the dean does not have the answers.

If you have information about any of the questions that are asked on the dean's certification, don't hesitate to share it with the person completing the form. That person can decide whether or not to use the information when responding to the questions.

Every school has its own office that handles dean's certifications. It may be the registrar's office or the university's dean of students or the dean of your college. If you're not sure who fills out these forms at your school, ask your advisor. If your advisor doesn't know and can't tell you where to go, ask the registrar's office.

A dean's certification is treated like a letter of recommendation in the sense that the person completing the form may send it directly to the school or give it to you in a sealed envelope to be included with your application when you mail it in.

Personal Statement/Essay

Many schools will require you to write a personal statement or an essay as part of the admissions process. (I will use *personal statement* and *essay* interchangeably in this section. Schools might also call them a *statement of purpose* or a candidate's *admission statement.*) Some schools will require more than one of these essays. In some cases, this is the most important part of your application. It is certainly the part over which you have the most control at the moment of your application, since your test scores and grades have already been received, your life experiences have already happened, and you have limited control over what is said in your letters of recommendation.

Perhaps because people have so much control over their personal statement, it is often the part of the application that intimidates them the most. By reading the information in this section, you should be able to write a compelling personal statement that will help, not hinder, your chances for admission.

When an admissions committee reads your personal statement, it is looking to see how well you write and how well you think. You don't need to use jargon or big, impressive-sounding words to show that you are a good writer. Clear, concise prose works quite well. What you choose to write about and how you write about it will show a committee how your mind works.

Some schools will ask you specific questions that must be answered in your essay. Others will leave the essay topic open-ended and will allow you to select the subject. No matter which approach a school takes, remember that the committee's ultimate objective in reading the essay is to evaluate your writing and thinking skills.

If you are asked to respond to a specific question, try to think of a response that won't be shared by 95 percent of the other applicants to that program. If you're asked why you're applying to medical school, saying that you want to help people is not a very original answer. Similarly, if asked why you're applying to law school, the response that you want to change the world by working on behalf of disenfranchised people is fairly common. If you feel like the only true response to a question will be shared by many other applicants, you will have to make your essay very persuasive, so the admissions committee will know that the answer you have given is heartfelt given your unique background and history, and is not just a cliché written because you don't know what else to say.

You may be asked to write two or three essays, each on a specific topic. All of the essays will be read by the admissions committee, so take advantage of this chance to tell the committee about different aspects of yourself. If you are given the chance to write an essay on an optional question, and the response to that question is contained somewhere else in your application, you probably don't want to respond to the optional question. If you can think of something fresh to include in the optional essay, that's great. Otherwise, redundancy isn't helpful to an admissions committee.

Follow the directions given for writing the essay. If you are asked to write about one important trait, then only write about one, not two or three. Admissions committees are judging how well you can follow directions and how well you can make distinctions and hard choices. You may often be faced with situations in life where you are asked for one response, but you want to give two or three. Your essay shows that you are capable of making those hard choices.

When writing your essay, think about the image you want the admissions committee to have of you when its members have finished reading your essay.

Do you want them to think you are intelligent? Funny? Courageous? Likable? Write with that theme in mind.

Use descriptive language and anecdotes to make your points. Telling how you traveled through India alone for six months, without speaking any of the Indian dialects, tells more about your determination and ability to adapt to difficult circumstances than just saying, "I am determined and can adapt easily."

Use your essay to include something that can't be found in the rest of your application. Your essay is not the place to give a prose version of your résumé or to reiterate information that can be gleaned from elsewhere in the application.

Make your essay credible. Although it may be true that your spring break spent volunteering with the poor changed your life, it is unlikely that one week dramatically altered your life. It is more believable to talk about the impact of that week on your thoughts and actions and perhaps show how it contributed to your growth and maturation process.

Accentuate the positive in your essay, and don't dwell on the negative. A personal statement is definitely not the place to make excuses or whine about all of the terrible things that have happened to you in the past. If you have a weak spot in your application that you think deserves explanation, it may be better to include that explanation in a separate addendum rather than putting it into your personal statement. Recognize that there is a difference between making excuses and stating facts. Most schools want to know if you have overcome obstacles in your life, so that is an appropriate topic for a personal statement. The key is to watch your language and the tone you use.

If you have a history of doing poorly on standardized tests and you have done poorly on the standardized test you took for graduate or professional school, you might want to document your history of test-taking. You can do this in a separate addendum and can state what your previous standardized test scores were and then show that they were not an accurate predictor of your academic success by correlating them with your grades.

Most schools will give you a recommended length for your essays or will tell you that they cannot exceed a certain length. If a school has a maximum length, exceed that length at your own risk. Some members of an admissions committee will simply stop reading an essay once it goes over the maximum length, especially if the essay is not very compelling reading to begin with.

Don't try to get around the length requirement by using a smaller font or narrower margins. A dense-looking essay is not going to put a file reviewer in a positive frame of mind. She wants to be able to read the essay easily and not have to squint or make her eyes travel across an exceedingly long line of text. Presentation does matter, so select a font that is appealing and easy to read.

It is usually ineffective to start your essay with a quotation from someone else. Admissions committees care what you think and how you write, not how someone else thinks and writes. Too often, a quote is a crutch for someone who doesn't know how else to start the essay.

A similar crutch is using an unusual format, like a poem or a recipe for success, or an essay in the form of an interview, or in the case of law school, an essay that reads like a legal brief. Although you want your essay to be memorable, you don't want it to be memorable for the wrong reasons.

Above all, make your essay original. You may be tempted to try to find other personal statements to see what "works." The danger of this is that you will try to copy the format or tone, and it won't work for you, because you are very different from the person who wrote the other personal statement. There is no formula for writing an essay. Many styles work well and lead to an admissions decision.

It is difficult to be funny in an effective way in a personal statement. I have read some funny personal statements that were very effective, but more often, I have read personal statements that attempted to be funny but were unsuccessful. Unless you have done a lot of writing using a "funny" style and have universally received acclaim for it, don't try it in your personal statement.

Before you start writing your personal statement, it may be helpful for you to sit down and review your résumé and make a list of all of the significant things you have done in your life. Then think about whether there are any themes that run through these experiences and whether one of them is an appropriate theme for your statement.

Treat your personal statement as if it were a class assignment and revise it a number of times until you are certain it conveys the message you think is important. Part of your revision process should include a careful proofreading of the statement to ensure that it has no typographical or grammatical errors.

Once you are happy with your statement, it's a good idea to let someone else read it. Most people will pick someone who knows them well. While that is fine, that person will be more likely to assume that he knows what you mean because he knows you so well. It can be more instructive to pick someone who doesn't know you well, since the members of the admissions committee who will be reading your statement also won't know you well. You can ask this person to tell you what impression he has of you after he reads the statement. If he has the impression you were trying to convey, congratulations, you're done. If he has a different impression, you need to find out why and try to change the statement to make it more closely reflect your ideas.

Include your name and Social Security or identification number on each page of your personal statement. Admissions offices are dealing with many pieces of paper, and if one page of your statement gets separated from your file, you want the office to be able to put it back in the proper place.

Interviews

Some programs will require an interview as part of the admissions process. Others will allow you to interview but don't require it. Still others will meet with interested applicants but will not consider that meeting during the admissions process. Schools that conduct interviews may ask all applicants to interview or they may only ask the candidates who have survived the first screening to come in. Alternatively, schools may ask just the borderline candidates to come in for an interview. If you fall into the latter category, it means that the admissions committee wants to give you an opportunity to explain a particular weakness in your application or the committee thinks you may be admissible and wants to give you a chance to prove or disprove that assumption.

If a school requests only selected applicants to interview, your invitation means that your interview may well be decisive in the admissions process.

Unless a school requires an interview of everyone, if you are asked to interview, you should strongly consider taking advantage of the opportunity. The only reason not to do so would be if you think you will make a poor impression in an interview. Unfortunately, most people vastly overrate their interviewing skills, so it may be hard for you to assess whether your interview will actually help or hurt you. You may want to try to get some objective advice on this subject.

Some schools will only conduct interviews on campus, while others will fly admissions officers to other cities to conduct interviews or will use alumni interviewers. Some schools may also be willing to conduct telephone interviews, although it can be particularly difficult for an interviewee to shine in these.

One applicant was invited to interview with my school, but he couldn't afford the plane fare and the time away from work to come clear across the country. As we talked, it turned out that I was going to be a couple of states away from him for a business trip, and he was able to fly there, so we arranged to interview in the airport.

On-campus interviews may be with a faculty member, an admissions officer, or a current student, who has usually been selected through a competitive process and has received special interview training. No matter who your interviewer is, that person's opinion will count, so accord that person proper respect.

If you meet a receptionist while you are coming or going from an interview, treat that person well. While she may not have any formal role in the admissions process, if you make an extremely positive or negative impression on her, she may share that with the admissions committee and that information could be taken into account when an admissions decision is being made.

The same is true for anyone else you might meet during the day, including students who take you on a tour or go to lunch with you. You don't want to be obsequious, neither do you want to be rude. Sometimes applicants think that they only have to be nice to those who they deem to be "important," like the chair of the department or the head of the admissions office. You need to treat everyone well and not discount someone just because his or her title sounds insignificant to you.

George came for an interview and was extremely articulate and thoughtful. The chair of the admissions committee was quite impressed. She heard later, though, that he was demanding and rude to the admissions staff. This caused her to revise her opinion of him.

If the schools to which you are applying don't require interviews but will allow them, you should think about whether the interview will enhance your chances of admission enough to be worth the time and money involved. As mentioned previously, try to do an honest assessment of your interview ability and don't just assume that you will make a positive impression.

Ask someone you trust to do a mock interview with you and ask you the types of questions that you might be asked in a real interview.

It is important to prepare for an interview and not to think that you can just go in and talk off the top of your head. You will be evaluated on everything from what you say to what you wear and how you shake hands. The following are the types of considerations that are often made by an interviewer.

- Your dress and personal appearance
- Your communication skills
- Your intellectual ability
- Your personality
- Your maturity level
- Your suitability for the program you are applying to
- Your motivation, drive, and determination

- Your emotional stability
- Your outside interests and activities
- An overall reaction

Your Dress and Personal Appearance

If you are interviewing for an MBA program, it is particularly important that you wear a suit and look the part of a business professional. If you are interviewing for another type of program, you may be able to dress more casually, as long as you are neatly attired, which means polished shoes and no clothes with holes in them. Jeans, tennis shoes, sweatshirts, or t-shirts would not be a good choice to wear to an interview.

You should be well groomed, which means the obvious, such as you should not have body odor, your breath should be clean-smelling, and your hair should be freshly washed. If you are a woman, your make-up and jewelry should be discreet.

Interviewers will form an instant impression of you based on what you look like and how you are dressed, and that impression can color the rest of the interview, so take care to make their first impression a good one.

Your Communication Skills

Your communication skills are one of the most important aspects of the interview. Interviewers want to know how well you can articulate your thoughts. Some programs may have room for brilliant students who can't communicate very well with others, but most want brilliant students who can work well with others.

The need for communication skills is obvious, both in the classroom and in your future career. If you want to be a teacher, you have to be able to communicate with your students; if you intend to be a doctor, you have to know how to talk to your patients; if law is your chosen career, you will have to communicate with clients and potentially juries and judges; as a businessperson, you will need to be able to communicate with others in the company, clients, suppliers, and a host of others.

If you hesitate a lot in conversation or you have many "uhs" and "ums" in your speech, you should try to rid yourself of those traits. Maintain good eye contact during the interview, and engage in a conversation with the interviewer. Don't just let the conversation be question, answer, question, answer. By preparing carefully ahead of time, you should be able to anticipate at least the types of questions that will be asked of you and you should have good answers ready for those questions.

Try to stay relaxed in an interview, so you don't appear too tense, but appear confident and certain when you speak. Taking deep breaths prior to the interview can help to clear your mind and slow your heart rate.

Your Intellectual Ability

Although interviewers generally don't expect you to have any particular substantive knowledge, they are using the interview to determine how intelligent you are and how well you can convey your knowledge to others. Are you brilliant but arrogant? Did you do well in school because you worked very hard, but you don't have much native intelligence? These are the types of questions interviewers will be trying to answer. They're looking for evidence of deep rather than superficial thinking. Since you are seeking to enter an academic community, your intellectual ability will be of great interest to an admissions committee.

Your Personality

Schools are looking for students who will fit in with the other students who are already enrolled. Since each school has its own type of student body, schools may be looking for different types of personalities. The best way to do well in an interview and to let your personality shine through is to go in feeling enthusiastic. Prepare by thinking about why you are applying to that particular program at that school. That thought process alone should kindle your enthusiasm. If it doesn't, you might ask yourself why you are going through the application process.

Your Maturity Level

Schools want students who have gotten beyond the desire to attend frequent drinking parties and who have a mature perspective on the program and the profession they plan to enter. You can demonstrate maturity by talking about responsibilities you have assumed, your plans for the future, and other topics that show you are a thoughtful person.

Your Suitability for the Program

This criterion seems obvious. Interviewers are trying to determine whether you are suitable for the program at their school. This can range from the broad issue of whether the interviewer thinks you are suitable for the profession you are entering to the narrower question of whether you are suitable for the particular school to which you are applying. It may be that the interviewer thinks you will be a fine doctor but doesn't think you are right for her program, which focuses on producing academic doctors. The more you understand about the nature of the program to which you are applying and the profession you plan to enter, the better you will be able to convince the interviewer that you are suitable for that program.

Your Motivation, Drive, and Determination

These traits are best demonstrated by past actions. You can prepare for questions relating to your motivation, drive, and determination by thinking about times in the past when you have exhibited these characteristics. Getting through a long graduate or professional program can be grueling, and interviewers want to know that you will not give up just because the program gets demanding.

Your Emotional Stability

Interviewers have similar reasons for wanting to know about your emotional stability. They are concerned about how well you will cope when the stress of your program builds. They recognize that their programs are stressful, and they want to admit students who will be able to handle that stress in appropriate ways.

Your Outside Interests and Activities

Interviewers may look at your outside interests because you will be part of a larger community. Schools want students who will add to the vitality of the class. Often they are looking for leaders because they anticipate that those students will initiate new activities or programs at the school and will also continue established programs and activities. Be ready to show that you are a well-rounded person who has done more than watch TV and attend classes.

An Overall Reaction

This category includes all of the categories discussed above plus other factors that come into play for an individual interviewer, either consciously or subconsciously. This is the bottom line where the interviewer has to make a decision as to whether you are a good fit for the program and will add to the program if you are admitted.

An often overlooked part of the interview is the importance of having good questions to ask the interviewer. The nature of the questions you ask can tell an interviewer a good deal about many of the characteristics listed above. Asking insightful questions that show you have thought about the program you are about to enter can make a strong impression. Conversely, asking questions that are answered in the school's bulletin shows that you are not very prepared and perhaps not very serious about the school.

Confirm your interview time and location a few days before the interview. Also ask about parking. Give yourself plenty of time to find the location, as campuses can be large and confusing.

Transcript

Every program will require you to submit a transcript as part of the admissions process. Schools usually will require an *official* transcript (a photocopy won't work) to be sent by your undergraduate, and graduate, if applicable, institution directly to the school. The exception is if you are applying to law school or medical school. The next two sections talk about how transcripts are handled for those two programs.

You should request your transcript in writing from the registrar's office. Some schools provide walk-up computers where you enter your request for a transcript and it is mailed within a couple of days. At other schools, you may submit an e-mail, fill out a form provided for that purpose, or send a letter. Be sure to include the name and address of the schools that should receive the transcripts, as well as the appropriate fee. Schools usually charge a fee for each transcript (the average charge is about $5.00). Because it may take up to a month for some schools to send your transcripts, you should submit your request in plenty of time for the transcript to be received by the deadline date.

A transcript will often show whether you have been on the dean's list or have been placed on academic probation, although these practices vary from school to school. The transcript will also usually indicate whether you had a declared major, so if you changed majors during school, both majors will appear.

When evaluating your transcript, admissions committees are looking for any grade trends. If you have not had consistently high grades throughout college, it is good if your grades improved. It is not good if you had a downward grade trend. If you had any dips in your performance, that is a signal to the committee to look more closely at your transcript. Perhaps your record is good except for one semester. If there is a reason for your poorer performance that semester, you may want to explain it to the admissions committee in an addendum to your personal statement.

An upward grade trend is very positive, while a downward grade trend requires some explanation.

The admissions committee will also look at the rigor of your course selection, the types of courses you have taken, and your major. As you will see in Chapter 6, the admissions committee isn't necessarily looking for a specific major but is looking for a rigorous major. The quality of the college you attended will also be considered when your transcript is examined. The more respect an admissions committee has for the rigor of your undergraduate institution, the more heavily the committee will weigh your academic performance.

Law School

If you are applying to law school, you will have your transcript sent directly to Law Services. Law Services will verify that it has received an official transcript and that it has received a transcript from every institution you have previously attended. Law Services will photocopy your transcript and will send it with your LSAT score to every law school to which you apply.

As part of its service, Law Services will also translate your transcript into a common system. Since schools use different grading scales (an A = 6 at some schools, and other schools use numbers instead of letters), Law Services standardizes the grades to make them all equivalent to a 4.0 scale. This sometimes results in the Law Services' GPA being different than the GPA reported by your school. Law schools will get your actual transcript and will see your school's calculated GPA, but they will also get Law Services' GPA.

Your grades will be reported on a standard summary sheet that will show the number of each letter grade you received each year. There will also be a GPA calculated each year, as well as a summary GPA that includes all undergraduate work. Your cumulative GPA will reflect only the grades earned at the institution where you received your degree.

Medical School

If you are applying to medical school, you will have your undergraduate institution send your transcript directly to AMCAS. AMCAS will send a copy of your transcript with your application and MCAT scores to each school to which you apply.

Standardized Test Scores

Chapter 3 talked extensively about the process of taking standardized tests and about the scoring scale used on each test, but how is the test score actually used in the admissions process? Many people believe that a standardized test score is the only factor used in the admissions process and want to give up in despair if they don't score well on the test. Although test scores are an important part of the process, their importance will vary from program to program and school to school.

Business schools that are primarily considering applicants who have been in the work world for a period of time doing similar work to what they will be doing with an MBA often will place more emphasis on that work experience than on a GMAT score. Some graduate programs also may place less emphasis on your GRE score than on other aspects of your application.

As a rule, law schools and medical schools will place more emphasis on standardized test scores. For the majority of schools, however, this does not mean that you will be denied admission based solely on your test score. Schools will still look at your entire application to see if there is good reason to place less weight on your test score and more weight on the other factors in your file.

If you have a strong application except for your standardized test score, don't assume that all schools will reject you just because of your score.

When you registered to take the GRE, GMAT, or MCAT, you indicated at that time which schools should receive your scores, so they will be sent automatically to those schools. You don't have to do anything else at this point unless you change your mind about where you are applying. If you are applying to law schools, the schools will request your LSAT score from Law Services after they receive your application. All you have to do is make sure that you have paid Law Services the correct fee for the number of schools to which you have applied.

Submitting Additional Materials

You may wonder whether it would be to your advantage to submit materials with your application other than those that were requested or required. You should do so cautiously. Admissions committees are already reading numerous pieces of paper and don't want to be burdened with extra paper that adds nothing to their deliberations. If the committee wanted to read a thesis from everyone, it would have asked for one. Instead of demonstrating your outstanding writing, an additional writing sample may cause a file reviewer to wonder if you lack confidence in your writing and are submitting an additional piece for that reason. You definitely do not need to submit a copy of your Phi Beta Kappa certificate or other honors and awards you have received; simply listing them in the appropriate place on your application is sufficient.

Typically, the most useful piece of additional information would mention something you feel needs explanation that is not covered in the rest of your application. Previous sections of this chapter talked about how you might want to include an addendum to your application if you have a history of poor standardized test-taking or you need to explain something about your grades.

Auditions

Music, theater, and dance programs may require an audition as part of the admissions process. If an audition is required, it will probably be the most important part of the admissions process. If you are unable to attend an audition, you can ask if you can submit a taped performance instead, but even if this is allowed, it is clearly not to your advantage. Each program will tell you what kind of material is appropriate for the audition, how long it should be, and other items you need to know.

Portfolios

Some graduate programs will require you to submit a portfolio as part of the application process. Programs most likely to request a portfolio are architecture, journalism, and art, including design. The portfolio shows your talent in the area you wish to study. Like an audition, a portfolio may be the most important factor in the admissions process. Programs will tell you what kinds of materials they expect in a portfolio and whether they should be presented in a particular way. You may be asked to present your portfolio as part of an interview.

How the Admissions Process Works

So what really happens after you have gathered all of the required information and submitted it to schools and are sitting back anxiously waiting for an answer? Are the schools randomly sorting applications and picking every third one to admit or are they engaged in a careful decision-making process? Who actually makes the admission decisions? This section will give you insight into these questions.

Admissions processes vary greatly from school to school, so this section should be used as a general guideline and a starting point that you can use to help you figure out the specifics of any particular school's admission process.

Schools will look at all of the information you have submitted and evaluate it in the ways that have been discussed in this chapter. The initial starting point for most schools is your GPA, your standardized test score, and other objective factors. Some people will form an initial impression of your admissibility based on these objective factors and will use the subjective factors to confirm or change their initial opinion.

Schools may use an *admissions index* or *formula* that assigns a certain weight to your GPA and to your standardized test score and then combines them to produce a third number, the index. An index might also include a component that factors in the quality of your undergraduate institution. Indexes can make it easier to compare candidates with different numbers to determine how similar they are.

Use of an index can show a school that Candidate A with a 3.6 GPA and a 2000 on the GRE is actually quite similar to Candidate B who has a 3.4 GPA and a 2250 on the GRE.

Some schools will group applications according to quality (based on your numbers) and will read the top applications first, working their way down to the bottom. Some schools have a cut-off point and won't review applications that are below a certain level. Others will read every application, although those with very low numbers may be given a more cursory examination than those with higher numbers.

Admissions Committee

Many schools use the phrase "admissions committee" throughout the admissions process, and your admit or deny letter may even say, "The admissions committee has decided . . ." Who sits on this mysterious admissions committee, and how does the committee make its decisions? Admissions committees may be composed of admissions office staff members, faculty members, and/or students. There also may be an admissions committee that sets policy, but the actual admissions decisions may be made by one person, typically a dean or director of admissions or a faculty member.

In some cases, each member of the admissions committee may be given a certain number of files to read. When the committee meets, that person presents the files he or she has read to the rest of the committee. In other cases, all members of the committee may read the applications independently and then vote on them, with the final vote being tallied by the admissions office. Another scenario would be for most decisions to be made by the admissions office, with only borderline files sent to committee members.

Some schools encourage or allow members of the admissions committee, especially if they are faculty members, to be as idiosyncratic as they like. This means that whether you are admitted may well depend on who reads your file. Even if a school tries to have each member of the admissions committee apply consistent standards, all file reviewers will come to the process with their own personal biases that may affect their opinions of your file.

A school usually has more than enough qualified applicants to fill every seat in the class. Thus, the admissions committee is looking for particular reasons to deny or admit someone. It's easy to deny you if you have a poorly written personal statement, your recommendations are negative, or you clearly aren't prepared for the program you want to pursue. The decision to admit you may not be so simple, even if you have an outstanding record of achievement, because lots of other applicants may also have outstanding records. That's where all of the subjective factors, like your personal statement, the enthusiasm you have shown throughout the process, your letters of recommendation, the previous contacts you have had with the department, and the unique qualities you will bring to the program come into play.

There are some special considerations for the admissions process if you are applying to graduate school or to medical school. They are covered in the following sections.

Graduate School

If you are applying to graduate school, your file may be reviewed by both the department and the graduate college. Typically, you will find that the department will make the admission decision, and the graduate college will process the paperwork and send the official notice of admission, although the graduate college may be responsible for all decisions. Because graduate school admissions usually is bifurcated between departments and the graduate college, you should make sure that you are sending materials to the proper offices.

Antonia was applying to graduate programs in English. At one school, she had to send all required documents to the graduate college. At another school, she sent her application to the graduate college, but she had to submit an additional writing sample directly to the English department. At the third school, she submitted everything to the English department.

Medical School

After medical schools receive your applications from AMCAS, they will make a preliminary determination as to who they would like to consider further. They will notify you if you are in the group that is still being reviewed and may ask you to submit additional information, including an application fee. After that information is received and reviewed, each school will decide whether to invite you for an interview.

Complete Files

A school won't review your application until it is complete, which means that all information has been received. Schools will determine the date of receipt, not by the date when you submitted the application form, but by the date when the last piece of required information was received.

What happens if a school receives a letter of recommendation for you before you have submitted your application form? The school will start a pending file for you and will match the letter of recommendation with the rest of your materials when they arrive. That's why it's best to make sure that your name and Social Security number are on every piece of paper that is submitted.

When to Call

If you know that your file is complete but you haven't received a decision, try to restrain your anxiety and not call the school. Your call usually won't do anything to speed up the process, and in fact, will just take time away from the admissions staff being able to process applications. If you must call, limit yourself to one phone call, and be courteous and brief.

If a school has given you a specific date by which it plans to mail its admission decisions, and you have not received a letter by a week after that date, you might call to find out if the letters have been mailed, and if not, when they anticipate mailing them. Even if a letter has been mailed, many schools will not give a decision out over the telephone, so you will just have to be patient and wait.

"Specials"

All schools have some applicants to which they might give special treatment during the admissions process. Some schools will give a preference to a legacy (an applicant whose parent graduated from that school). This often is true at private schools more than public schools and may mean that if a candidate is otherwise qualified, she may be admitted in lieu of another candidate with similar qualifications. Other candidates may be given preferential treatment because an alumnus has recommended them, a faculty member has recommended them, or their parents have made a large contribution to the school. Public schools may be susceptible to pressure from state officials. Typically, any type of preference is just one additional piece of information that is considered when your application is reviewed, and you are by no means guaranteed admission.

Rolling Admissions

Some schools use a rolling admissions process where they review applications as they are received and send out decisions throughout the cycle. Rolling admissions usually does not mean the applications will be reviewed in the exact order in which they were received, i.e., an application received on November 1 won't necessarily be read before an application that was received on November 2. What it means is that applications received about the same time will be read about the same time.

If a school uses rolling admissions, it is generally to your advantage to submit your application early in the process. That way, you will be considered before the class is full, and you will receive a decision earlier in the process. At the very least, you want to make sure that your application is not received on or just prior to the deadline. The reason for that is the school may have filled all of its spaces by the time it gets to your application, so no matter how good you are, you won't be admitted.

Non-Rolling Admissions

There are a couple of common models that are used by schools that don't use rolling admissions. Business schools tend to use admission *rounds*, where they separate the admissions period into separate rounds. All applications that are received during a round are grouped together and read at the same time. Decisions are mailed to all of those applicants at the end of the round.

Schools may also wait until after the application deadline to start reading any files. They may start with the best files first or they may work from both ends (best applicants and worst applicants) to reach the middle. Decisions typically are sent as decisions are made, so schools are not waiting for a particular date to mail your decision.

When You'll Get Your Decision

As demonstrated in the previous sections on rolling and non-rolling admissions, the timing of when you will receive your decision will vary. Unless you are applying to an early action program, you probably will receive your decision sometime in the spring (January through April). You will usually not have to respond to the offer until sometime in April or May, after you have received financial aid decisions from every school.

Decisions You Might Receive

There are three decisions you can receive from a school: admit, waitlist, or deny. We'll cover each of those in turn.

Admit

If you receive an admit decision, congratulations! You can read Chapter 9 about how to choose a school after you have been admitted. Once you choose the school you want to attend (try to make your decision as quickly as possible), you should immediately notify all other schools that have admitted you that you are turning down their offers. Most schools want to know where you plan to attend because it helps them gauge their competition, so don't be offended if you are asked.

Waitlist

If you are put on the waitlist, this means that you will be considered again for admission if someone else who has been admitted turns down the offer of admission. Waitlist decisions can be made anytime from April until the day before classes start. Being patient while remaining on a waitlist can be extremely difficult for some people. They think that if they call every day during the summer, they will miraculously be offered a position in the class.

While it is good to let a school know that you remain interested in the school, it is not wise to make a pest of yourself. Calling, sending an e-mail, or writing a letter about once a month is usually sufficient to let the school know that you are still interested and would be willing to take a spot in the class if it were offered to you. Don't let your ego get in your way by trying to be admitted to a school just for its prestige value, even though you have already decided to go somewhere else and won't change your mind even if admitted to the other school.

If a school offers you a position on the waitlist and you no longer wish to attend that school, you should contact the school and politely say that you do not wish to be kept on the waitlist. Schools will appreciate your letting them know, as will other candidates who wish to remain on the waitlist.

Jessica desperately wanted to attend the school where I worked. She called constantly and said that she would come at any point if she was admitted. On orientation day, she showed up and said that she wanted me to know that she was staying at a nearby motel and planned to be there all week in case someone didn't show up for orientation or decided to drop out after classes had started. She even gave me a check for the first semester's tuition just to prove that she was serious. She was a bit obnoxious and demanding. She asked if she could attend orientation, just in case she was admitted. I told her no. She then found out where the first-year students were going out that evening, and she joined them. She told them that she hoped she would be admitted and that's why she was there. They found it a bit strange and reported it to me. I told her to go home, because she wasn't going to be admitted, even if someone did drop out.

Mark was another student who was on the waitlist who wanted very much to attend my school. He showed up on orientation day and said very politely that he was there just in case someone else didn't show up. He wanted us to know that he was very interested in the school and would be willing to take a place that opened up. He was courteous and professional, and if a place had opened up, he probably would have received it, because he was there, his credentials were good, and he acted appropriately.

Deny

If you are denied, you may have received offers from other schools that will meet your needs just as well, so you will also go to Chapter 9 to read about choosing among offers. If, however, you have been rejected from every school or you have been rejected from the one school you really want to attend, you have to ask yourself whether you want to reapply the following year.

If you are rejected from every school, you should take a hard look at yourself to determine if you are suited for the program you are pursuing. Unless you applied only to extremely competitive schools, there probably is a good reason why you weren't admitted anywhere. Try to figure out that reason and if there is any way to overcome it. If there isn't, you might decide at this point to redirect your goals and plans for the future.

If you applied to extremely competitive schools, you can change the mix of schools to which you applied. Reread Chapter 4 on deciding where to apply, and pay particular attention to the section on choosing safety and middle schools.

If you applied to a school you really want to attend, you could try contacting the school to see if there is any reason why you weren't admitted. Take what you are told with a grain of salt, though. Schools may be reluctant to tell you the real reason why you were denied, or they may be unable to give you a concrete reason. The latter typically happens when the school has received a large number of applications from highly qualified people, and there was no particular reason why others were chosen over you. If a school does give you a reason for your denial, don't try to argue about whether that reason was valid. Just accept it and decide if it is something you can change for the next year.

Early Action Options

Some schools may offer early action options, where if you apply by a certain date, you will receive a decision by a certain date. Some medical schools offer an early decision program, where you can apply to only one school and must apply by August 1. Your admission decision will be mailed by October 1, and you must accept the offer if you are admitted. You should take advantage of this option only if you are very interested in a certain school and you think your chance of being admitted there is quite high. The risk is that you won't be admitted and won't know until after October 1, and then will have to apply to other medical schools. Since that is relatively late in the admissions process, your chances of admission will decrease at those other schools.

The process is a little easier for law schools, since you can apply to as many law schools as you like without penalty, even if you are applying to some schools early action. The number of law schools that offer early action options is relatively small but is growing. One law school requires early action applicants to accept the school's offer if they are admitted and to withdraw from consideration by other schools. All other law schools that offer early action options allow applicants to continue to apply and be admitted to other schools. The advantage of a nonbinding early action option is that you can apply early and get a decision early and then decide whether you want to apply to other schools. If you are happy with the school where you are admitted, you don't need to go to the time, trouble, and expense of completing additional applications.

Timelines for Applying

Application timelines will vary from program to program and individual to individual. Some people will want to do everything well in advance, while others will feel more comfortable leaving things until a bit later in the process. The following sections will give you a starting point for planning your own schedule of what you should be doing when for the application process for each type of program. The timelines assume that you will be starting school in the fall. If you plan to start school at some other point during the year, you should adjust the timelines accordingly.

Medical School

Two Years Before You Plan to Attend

- ❒ September—Schedule a meeting with your pre-medical adviser to talk about the admissions process.
- ❒ October–January—Begin doing some preliminary preparation for the MCAT.
- ❒ January—Request the MCAT registration booklet.
- ❒ February—Register for the MCAT and talk to your pre-medical adviser about getting letters of recommendation.
- ❒ February–April—Prepare extensively for the MCAT.
- ❒ April—Take the MCAT.
- ❒ May—Request the application from AMCAS and request applications from schools that don't use AMCAS.
- ❒ May–June—Write your application essay and complete your applications. Tell your pre-medical adviser which schools should receive your letters of recommendation.
- ❒ June–August—Submit your applications. Most people submit their applications in July or August. The earliest application date at schools is either June 1 or June 15.

One Year Before You Plan to Attend

- ❒ September—Check with your pre-medical adviser to see if your recommendations have been sent to the schools.
- ❒ October—Contact the medical schools to make sure they have received your applications. If a school asks you to submit additional information, complete those forms and turn them in as soon as possible.
- ❒ November—Prepare for interviews.
- ❒ December–January—Interview with schools where you have been invited. Complete any requested supplemental applications.
- ❒ January—Get the Free Application for Federal Student Aid and complete and submit it. Check with schools to make sure your application is complete.
- ❒ January–February—If you are a senior in college and your first-semester grades are good, send your transcript to schools that have not sent you a decision.
- ❒ Spring—Receive your decision letters and decide where to attend. Check with the financial aid office to be sure your financial aid application is complete.

Business School

One Year Before You Plan to Attend

- ❒ August—Request applications from the business schools. Request the GMAT information booklet and think about how you will prepare for the GMAT.
- ❒ Fall—Attend MBA Forums held in cities throughout the country to learn more about different MBA programs.
- ❒ September—Register for the GMAT. Begin intensive preparations for the GMAT. Request transcripts from the schools you have attended. Ask the people who you would like to write letters of recommendation for you.
- ❒ October—Take the GMAT. Begin writing personal essays.

- ❒ November—Begin working on applications. Contact recommenders to remind them about upcoming deadlines.
- ❒ December—Submit completed applications to schools.
- ❒ December–March—Interview with schools.
- ❒ January—Get the Free Application for Federal Student Aid and complete and submit it. Check with schools to make sure your application is complete.
- ❒ January–February—If you are a senior in college and your first-semester grades are good, send your transcript to schools that have not sent you a decision.
- ❒ Spring—Receive your decision letters. If you did not have an interview at a school that admitted you, visit the school, talk to students and alumni, and make your decision. Check with the financial aid office to be sure your financial aid application is complete.

Law School

Two Years Before You Plan to Attend

- ❒ September–November—Attend law school information fairs held throughout the country to try to get a better idea of whether a law degree is right for you and what you are seeking in a law school.
- ❒ April–May—Request the LSAT preparation materials, register for the LSAT, and prepare for the LSAT.
- ❒ June—Take the LSAT.

One Year Before You Plan to Attend

- ❒ Summer—If possible, visit some of the schools that interest you. If you didn't register for LSDAS when you registered for the LSAT, register for it now.
- ❒ August—Request applications from law schools.
- ❒ September—Schedule a meeting with your pre-law adviser. Begin working on your personal statement. Request transcripts from the schools you have attended. Ask the people who you would like to write letters of recommendation for you.

- ❒ October—Begin working on your applications.
- ❒ September–November—Attend law school information fairs held throughout the country to get information about specific schools in which you are interested.
- ❒ November–December—Submit your applications. About one month before you plan to submit your application, remind your recommenders of upcoming deadlines.
- ❒ January—Get the Free Application for Federal Student Aid and complete and submit it. Check with schools to make sure your application is complete.
- ❒ January–February—If you are a senior in college and your first-semester grades are good, send your transcript to schools that have not sent you a decision.
- ❒ Spring—Receive your decision letters, visit the schools that admitted you and in which you are still interested, talk to students and alumni, and make your decision. Check with the financial aid office to be sure your financial aid application is complete.

Graduate School

Two Years Before You Plan to Attend

- ❒ Spring—Get catalogs from schools and find out their requirements for standardized tests (do they require the GRE General Test or the GRE Subject Test or both?). Get information about the GRE from ETS.

One Year Before You Plan to Attend

- ❒ Summer—Register for the GRE. Begin GRE preparation.
- ❒ August—Request applications from graduate schools. Be sure to contact the individual department and the graduate college.
- ❒ September—Begin working on your personal statement. Request transcripts from the schools you have attended. Ask the people who you would like to write letters of recommendation for you.

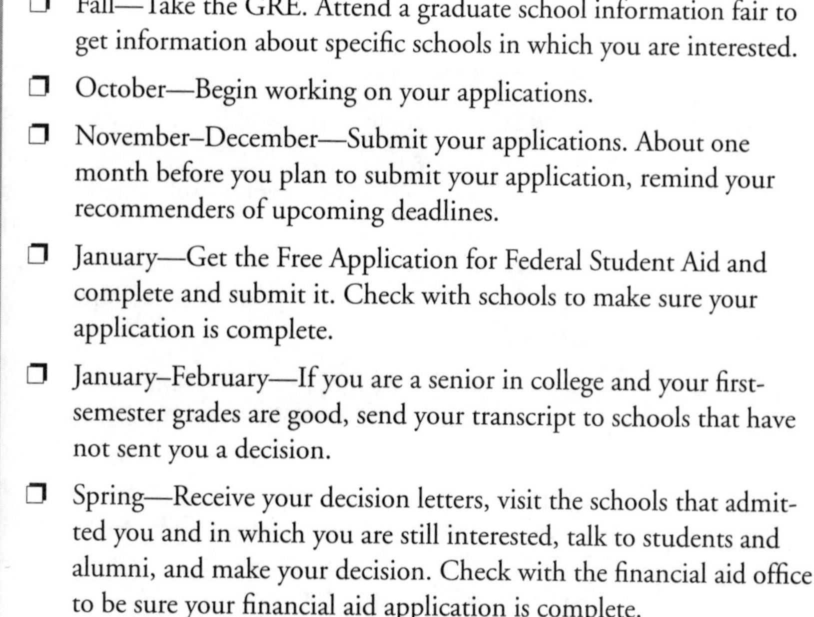

- ❒ Fall—Take the GRE. Attend a graduate school information fair to get information about specific schools in which you are interested.
- ❒ October—Begin working on your applications.
- ❒ November–December—Submit your applications. About one month before you plan to submit your application, remind your recommenders of upcoming deadlines.
- ❒ January—Get the Free Application for Federal Student Aid and complete and submit it. Check with schools to make sure your application is complete.
- ❒ January–February—If you are a senior in college and your first-semester grades are good, send your transcript to schools that have not sent you a decision.
- ❒ Spring—Receive your decision letters, visit the schools that admitted you and in which you are still interested, talk to students and alumni, and make your decision. Check with the financial aid office to be sure your financial aid application is complete.

Guidelines for the Application Process

If you follow the guidelines listed below, you will find that the application process will be much smoother for you.

1. Be organized. Establish a system for organizing the various documents needed for each school to which you are applying. See the appendix to this chapter for a chart you can use during this process. One applicant created a wall chart, with a checklist on it. Since it was always staring him in the face, it was hard to forget what he had to do when.
2. Put your name and Social Security number on every piece of paper you submit with your application. If a school does not provide a form for your recommenders to use, it is helpful to ask your recommenders to include your name and Social Security number in their letters of recommendation.
3. Keep a copy of everything you send to the admissions office.
4. Consider sending your application via registered or certified mail or using an express mail service, in order to verify that it was received.

5. If your address or phone number changes at any point during the admissions process, promptly notify the schools. The same is true for any other information that may change on your application.
6. Proofread your application carefully before you send it in. Schools often will receive a personal statement that says, "Please substitute this personal statement for the version I submitted previously. I discovered an error in the first version." Some schools will keep that letter and both versions of the personal statement in the file, so the admissions committee can use that additional piece of information in making its decision.
7. Treat the admissions office well. Recognize that they are dealing with many other applicants, and don't monopolize their time. You should definitely call if you have questions and can't find the answers in the written materials or on the Web site, but calling and asking for the school's application deadline shows either that you're lazy or that you haven't done your homework about that school and probably aren't very serious about it.
8. Meet the schools' deadlines for applications.
9. If, by one or two weeks after you have submitted your application, you have not received an acknowledgment that your file is complete, contact the school to find out if everything has been received. If an item is missing, make arrangements to get it submitted right away.

Misconduct in the Admissions Process

It should go without saying that you must conduct yourself with the utmost integrity during the admissions process. Cases of applicant misconduct range from answering "no" to a question about disciplinary actions being taken against you during college to a recent case reported in *The Chronicle of Higher Education*, where a Yale graduate student in neuroscience was charged with forging transcripts and letters of recommendation in order to be admitted.

Many applications will ask you about your prior conduct and will want to know if you have ever been arrested or have ever been disciplined by your university. Read these questions carefully and answer them truthfully and completely. Usually the omission of a prior disciplinary problem will cause more trouble than if you had just explained the situation. If you're not sure whether an incident in which you were involved was too minor to include when you are asked about such incidents on the application, call and ask the admissions office.

Forging any documents that you use in the admissions process is absolutely forbidden. If you are caught after you have been admitted, you will be expelled, no matter how brilliantly you are performing in the program. If you are caught before you have been admitted, you will be denied admission and your conduct may well be reported to other schools.

Offering to pay a school official money if you are admitted is another obvious case of misconduct that will keep you from being admitted. School officials are not susceptible to that type of persuasion.

Conclusion

By following the advice in this chapter, you will be able to approach the admissions process with confidence and to submit excellent applications that will enhance your chances of admission. Now you need to decide how you can best position yourself for admission to the schools of your choice. The next chapter will help you figure out the answer to that question.

Application Checklist

	School A	School B	School C
Application and Catalog			
Date Requested			
Date Received			
Standardized Test			
Date Materials Requested			
Materials Received Yet?			
Date of Test			
Scores Received by School?			
Application			
Application Deadline			
Application Fee			
Target Completion Date			
Interview			
Interview Date			
School Visit			
School Visit Date			
Transcripts			
Date Requested			
Received Yet?			
Personal Statement/Essay			
Target Completion Date			
Date Completed			

	School A	School B	School C
Recommendations			
Recommender 1			
Date Requested			
Date Information and Forms Provided			
Date Sent to School			
Received by School?			
Recommender 2			
Date Requested			
Date Information and Forms Provided			
Date Sent to School			
Received by School?			
Financial Aid			
Date Information Requested			
Date Received			
Deadline			
Date Sent			
Date FAFSA Completed			
Date SAR Received			
SAR Received by School?			
Date Loan Applications Completed			

chapter 6

Positioning Yourself for Admission

Now that you generally understand something about the admissions process, you need to think about how you can best position yourself to increase your chance of being admitted to the school of your choice. Whether you are currently in college or have already graduated, there are things you can do to enhance your marketability. Not all of the topics will apply to every program or to every person, so you should read this chapter with an eye toward what will work for you.

Since you have unique strengths and attributes as an applicant, you need to figure out how to capitalize on those assets and make them work to your advantage in the admissions process. Don't approach the admissions process with the mindset that says there are certain tasks that must be accomplished and if you accomplish them, you will be guaranteed admission. As you saw in the previous chapter, admissions committees are looking for diverse, interesting people who have had a wide variety of life experiences. They are not looking for everyone to be exactly the same. Thus, you need to determine what you can do to make yourself stand out. This chapter will discuss the following areas where you might be able to prepare yourself for admission:

- Choice of college
- Undergraduate major
- Coursework
- Foreign language
- Post-college work experience
- Internships/college work experience
- Extracurricular activities
- Community service
- Writing experience
- Getting to know your adviser

Choice of College

The strength of your undergraduate institution usually is a factor in the admissions process. If you have already graduated from college or are about to graduate, you obviously cannot change your college at this point. However, you can include information in your application about the quality of the school if your school is not very well known. You can ask one of the professors writing a letter of recommendation for you to mention others from your school who have successfully completed a program similar to the one to which you are applying. The professor can also talk about the quality of the students at that institution and the quality of the faculty. Some schools have a one-page information sheet that applicants can include with their application materials.

If you decide as a sophomore that you want to attend graduate school in English, and your college has a very small English department from which no one has ever gone on to graduate school, you might want to give serious thought to transferring to a school with a larger English department and that has had more students apply to graduate school.

Medical schools give a slight priority to students who have graduated from the university where that medical school is located. Statistics show that an applicant who attended a private undergraduate college has a better chance of being admitted to a private medical school. It is also helpful in the admissions process if you attended a college that has a good record of getting students admitted to medical school. The 1995 edition of *The College Handbook* states that the following universities report that 10 percent or more of their graduates go on to attend medical school:

- Brandeis University
- Brown University
- Columbia University
- Davidson College
- Duke University
- Emory University
- Harvard University
- Johns Hopkins University
- Massachusetts Institute of Technology (MIT)
- New York University
- Pomona University
- Stanford University
- Tufts University
- Washington University

Undergraduate Major

You may assume that if you want to attend medical school, you have to major in a science field or that if you want to attend law school, you have to major in political science, English, or another field in the social sciences or humanities. Perhaps you're thinking that you have to have an undergraduate degree in the same field in which you want to earn your master's degree or PhD. On the contrary, all of these programs are open to students who have a wide variety of majors. This is not to say that your choice of a major is unimportant, only that you are not as restricted as you might have thought you were. Keep in mind that although a particular major might not be required for a specific program, you may need to take certain types of courses in order to be considered a strong admissions candidate.

It is very helpful to take more than one class in your major from the same professor (and to do well in those classes), so that professor can write a letter of recommendation for you. Since the best letters of recommendation come from those people who know you the best, you can give a professor the opportunity to get to know you by taking more than one class from him or her. It's also helpful to get to know the professor outside of class by going to office hours or stopping and asking questions after class.

Some graduate and professional schools offer programs where you can get your bachelor's degree and your MD, MBA, or JD in a shorter amount of time than if you first got your bachelor's degree and then applied to professional school. BA/BS and MD programs are offered by 28 medical schools. You have to apply to the program when you are applying to college right out of high school and are admitted only if your record is truly exceptional. The length of the combined programs varies from six to eight years.

Business and law schools that offer combined degrees of this nature usually structure their programs so that you attend only three years of undergraduate school and then the normal number of years for business school or law school. Although some schools may admit students to these programs right out of high school, it is more common for students to apply to them while they are enrolled in college. Some business and law schools may offer this option only to students who are enrolled as undergraduates at their university, while others may accept students from other schools. If you are interested in this type of program, you should talk to an adviser and make plans at a very early stage in your college career.

The next sections will provide information about different graduate and professional school programs and their requirements regarding undergraduate majors.

Medical School

Common wisdom says that you can't be admitted to medical school unless you have majored in biology, chemistry, or some other aspect of the sciences, right? Wrong. Although it is important to take science courses while in college, medical schools do not require science majors as a condition of admission. In fact, because it is more unusual for a nonscience major to apply to medical school, you may be at a slight advantage in the admissions process if you decide not to major in a science. The American Association of Medical Colleges reports that in a recent year, just over 50 percent of history majors who applied to medical school were admitted, while just over 40 percent of students who majored in the physical sciences were admitted. While in medical school, nonscience majors do just as well as science majors.

Plan your science curriculum so you take the science courses needed for the MCAT prior to your senior year of college.

No matter what your major is, you should take the following courses prior to your senior year in order to prepare for the MCAT: one year of biology, one year of general and/or inorganic chemistry, one year of organic chemistry, and one year of physics. You should also read the medical school catalogs to see if they require any particular courses for admission. Most schools require applicants to have completed one year of biology, one year of inorganic chemistry, one year of organic chemistry, one year of physics, and one year of English. Nineteen medical schools require one year of calculus. If a school lists courses as desirable or recommended for admission, it's wise to take them and to do well in them.

If you earned Advanced Placement (AP) credits in science courses, it's still a good idea to take some college science classes in the same areas in which you got the AP credits, so the admissions committee can see your science background.

Law School

Law schools are looking for and admit students with all types of majors. Law schools admit music majors to physics majors and everything in between. When selecting a major for law school, it's wise to keep in mind that law schools are looking for evidence of your ability to think, read critically, analyze, and write. Any major that emphasizes those skills will be good preparation for law school.

Law school admissions committees are at least as interested in the intellectual rigor of the courses you have taken as they are in the major you have chosen. They also like to see that you have challenged yourself by taking courses in a broad array of areas, rather than being narrowly focused. A very few schools may offer a pre-law major. It is actually quite uncommon for law schools to receive applications from students who have majored in "pre-law," so don't think that you have to have that major in order to be admitted. Other schools may offer a pre-law curriculum that consists of suggested courses a pre-law student should take. These usually include English courses, a logic course, and other courses that require you to read text closely, analyze, and write.

Take the most challenging courses you can in a wide variety of subjects. Don't try to pad your GPA by taking "gut" or "crip" courses.

Many colleges now offer some type of undergraduate "law" course. Examples of these would be Legal Aspects of Business or Constitutional Law. While these may be interesting college courses, law schools will not place any more weight on them in the admissions process than they place on other courses you have taken. The reason for this is that undergraduate law courses are typically not similar in style or content to the courses you will take in law school. Thus, they are not a useful indicator of your law school performance.

Business School

Like medical schools and law schools, business schools don't have a preference as to a major. They know that many majors can prepare you quite well for the rigors of business school. They are looking for evidence of a demanding curriculum that includes a broad array of courses. Business schools also want to see some evidence of your quantitative abilities, so taking economics, statistics, and/or calculus will enhance your transcript and will help your performance in business school.

Statistics, economics, and calculus are good classes to take in preparation for business school.

Graduate School

Many graduate programs will tell you what preparation is best for that program, either by recommending a specific major or telling you what courses you should take. Requirements can vary greatly from program to program and from school to school. Graduate programs in the sciences are more likely to require you to have a major, or at least substantial courses, in the program you plan to pursue. Programs in the humanities and social sciences may have less stringent requirements regarding your undergraduate preparation.

Check early in the process with the schools you are considering to see if they require a particular major or specific courses for admission.

If you have already graduated from college and you didn't major in a field that is recommended or required for the graduate degree you want to pursue, is it too late? The answer is no. You may be able to take additional courses to help make up for any deficiencies. Coursework will be covered in the next section.

Coursework

The previous section talked about how you might select particular courses, apart from your major, to strengthen your application for certain programs. This section will focus on what you can do if you have already graduated and think you need additional preparation for the degree you want to pursue. Taking college courses on a part-time basis (many colleges offer courses at night for people who are working full-time) can be a great way to pursue the courses you didn't take during college but find that you now need for admission to graduate school.

Another option would be to quit your job and attend school full-time until you have completed the courses you need. If you need a large number of courses, this would clearly shorten the amount of time required to get them. The downside is that you could quit your job and put a lot of time into taking these courses and then find that you aren't admitted to the program for which you were preparing.

Sergei had an undergraduate degree and a master's degree in English. He had had many interesting jobs over the years, but in his 30s, he decided that he wanted to return to school and get a master's degree in physical therapy. Even with his extensive educational background, he hadn't taken the science courses that were recommended for admission. He also hadn't done well academically during his undergraduate years, preferring to party rather than study. He sold his business and went to college full-time for two years to get the requisite courses for admission to a master's program. He also volunteered at a local rehabilitation hospital to get experience. He got As in all of his courses and got good recommendations from his volunteer supervisors, and he was admitted to a good program .

You might want to take additional classes before applying to graduate or professional school, even if your major is suitable for the program that interests you. Taking extra classes would be advantageous if your undergraduate record is weak. Taking graduate-level classes in any subject, even if not for a degree, helps to show that you are now capable of doing high-quality scholarly work. The longer you have been out of college and the greater your record of achievement since college, the less you will need to worry about making up for academic weaknesses by taking classes. However, if your undergraduate record is weak and you have been out of college for just a few years or your track record since graduation is unimpressive, then you should seriously consider taking some classes to boost your chance of admission.

Some people will decide to pursue a graduate degree in a field with less stringent admissions requirements and will do well enough in that program that they can use those grades to help them get admitted to a professional school that is more difficult to get into. This can be a long and expensive process, however, and is usually not necessary. The better approach is simply to take courses, preferably at the graduate level, to show that you can do the work that will be required of you.

If you decide to take some additional courses, you should choose your college wisely. You may not have much choice in the situation, depending on your location and how many schools are located near you, but to the extent that you do have a choice, you should select the best school possible for your continuing coursework. It's not as impressive to an admissions committee if your work was done at a community college rather than at a four-year institution.

If you know that you would like to pursue a graduate degree at a particular school, you can apply there as a nondegree student and take some courses that show your abilities and your commitment. You will be able to get to know professors who are teaching in the program you want to enter, and that will help your chances of admission.

Some schools offer "probationary" programs where they will admit you to their program on a conditional basis. These programs typically start in the summer and you take two or three courses during that time that are the same as the courses you would be taking in the regular program. You are usually given extra attention by the professors and some extra help. If you succeed, you are then fully admitted to the program. If you don't succeed, you cannot continue in that program. These are good programs for people whose applications show that they are risky candidates but who appear to have the potential to do the work required.

If you decide after you have graduated from college that you want to attend medical school but you don't have the science background required, you can take science courses on your own, or you can look for one of the many schools that offer special programs specifically for people like you. These programs are designed to help college graduates who want to attend medical school meet the pre-medical school requirements.

Foreign Language

Many graduate programs in the humanities and social sciences will require you to have a strong background in a foreign language. This requirement may manifest itself as part of the admissions process, or it may be that you don't need to demonstrate your language proficiency until after you have graduated. Either way, if a school cares about languages, it can be helpful to your application to have taken at least some language courses prior to commencing your studies.

Some business schools and law schools will consider it a positive factor in your application if you are proficient in a foreign language. Since the international world tends to affect businesses, even in very unlikely places, some schools recognize that their graduates will have an advantage if they are familiar and comfortable with other cultures. These traits are often true of those who can speak a foreign language. If you are applying to law schools or business schools that have a strong international focus, even if you don't intend to work in the international arena, you will find that foreign-language ability will be a plus factor in your admissions application.

Post-College Work Experience

Post-college work experience is a necessity for most business schools. For other programs, although work experience is not required, it may aid your application, especially if it is the type of work that shows you have the ability to do well in the type of program to which you are applying. For example, if you are applying for a graduate degree in accounting or engineering, and you have worked after college, it will be helpful to your application if your work is in accounting or engineering. Obviously your work has to be high-quality in order to be beneficial. This type of work experience is especially useful if you majored in the field in which you want to get your graduate degree and you did poorly in that major.

Arthur went to a large, well-respected state university and performed terribly. He alternated semesters between flunking out and dropping out. He started working part-time during this period doing data entry. He then began working full-time doing more sophisticated computer work and was transferred out of state. Once he had moved, he decided to take advantage of his company's tuition reimbursement plan and to continue his undergraduate degree in computer science. The only school he could attend using the company's plan was a small, academically weak school. Although he got straight As in this program, he was concerned about how that would look compared to all of the Ds and Fs he had received from a school that was much stronger academically. He finally received his bachelor's degree ten years after starting it and he applied to graduate school in computer science. He was admitted based largely on his very significant work experience in the area. His later straight As also helped, but they alone might not have been enough to get him admitted, considering his previous poor performance in school.

If you are not sure whether you want to attend graduate or professional school or which degree you want to pursue, you should definitely try to get work in the area you are considering. Pay close attention to the people who are doing the type of work you might want to do to determine whether you would enjoy it. Look closely at their day-to-day activities and think about whether you want to spend your day in a similar manner.

Mary thought she wanted to be a professor because she would enjoy standing up in front of a classroom every day. Yet, when she looked closely at the life of a professor, she saw that very little of that person's time is actually spent in the classroom. A great deal of time is spent researching and writing, preparing for class, and engaging in faculty politics. Once she looked at the entire package, she was able to figure out that there were other professions where she could use the speaking skills that she enjoyed so much and where she wouldn't have to do the research that she didn't like.

If you are not trying to make up for a poor academic record and you just want to get some work experience between college and graduate or professional school, your choices are unlimited. Generally, schools like to see work where you have had to solve problems, think analytically, and interact with others. They also like to see that you assumed responsibility and that you advanced, through promotions or raises, if you were there for two or more years. You will have many years (30 or more) to work in the field in which you will earn your graduate or professional degree, so the time between college and getting that degree can be used to work in a completely unrelated field.

Business School

Business schools prefer you to have two to three years' experience working in some type of managerial or professional position before applying to an MBA program. The exact type of work doesn't matter, as long as you can demonstrate that you have gained the experiences admissions committees are seeking. Typically, they are looking to see whether you have been successful at your job, managed others, and demonstrated good interpersonal skills.

Common work experiences for pre-MBA students are being a consultant, investment banker, or accountant, working in the financial services industry, or working in marketing. Many companies in these areas hire college graduates with the expectation that they will work for them for a few years and then will apply to MBA school. Obviously, these career paths work or else they wouldn't be so popular. Yet, MBA schools don't want everyone to have the same kind of background.

Jed graduated from a private liberal arts college and then went to work for an investment bank for two years. He found that most of his co-workers planned to apply to MBA programs. About half of them were admitted after two years and half were not.

Since applications from people with the experiences mentioned above are common, you might want to make your application a bit more unusual by getting a different type of work experience. If you majored in engineering, you can work as an engineer for a few years; if you were a biology major, you can work in that field; an English major could work for a publishing company. The possibilities are unlimited, as long as you find work where you can be successful and can demonstrate the attributes business school admissions committees are looking for.

Luann joined the Peace Corps after graduating from a large state university. She worked in Africa for two years, and due to the difficulties of applying while she was abroad, she waited until she returned to the United States to apply to MBA programs. She spent the year after her return taking the GMAT, researching schools, and making her applications. She also had a part-time research position during that year. Her very thoughtful and carefully prepared application showed how important her Peace Corps experience was, and she was admitted to an MBA program.

Law School

It is not necessary, nor even necessarily desirable, for you to work in the legal profession before attending law school. While working for a district attorney's office, a law firm, or a public service agency might help you decide whether you want to attend law school and can be very valuable for that reason, prior legal work is not a criterion for admission to law schools. Law schools recognize that the work of most paralegals is not similar to the work of most lawyers, so that type of experience is not indicative of how well you will do in law school. However, if you work for a well-known, well-respected legal organization and you get a great letter of recommendation from an attorney there, that can convince an admissions committee to take a careful look at your application.

The type of work that will most enhance your application to law school is that which requires you to write, think analytically, interact with others, and solve problems. Since those traits can be demonstrated in a wide variety of jobs, you are not limited in the kind of work you should seek. Construction workers, elevator repair people, journalists, diplomats, businesspeople, teachers, musicians, engineers, and professional athletes are just some of the people who have gone on to law school.

Medical School

Since medical schools like to enroll younger students, they are not looking for applicants with significant work histories. Most medical schools prefer their students to be recent college graduates, with perhaps one or two years of work experience. They often will not admit students who are over 35 years old. If you are older and you want to apply to medical school, your chances of admission are better if you have worked in a field related to medicine, like being a physician's assistant or working in biomedical science. You will be less desirable to an admissions committee if you have established a career in a field completely unrelated to medicine.

If you are going to attend graduate or professional school right out of college and don't have the opportunity to work, are there any types of work experience you can have during college that will help your chances of being admitted? The next section will address that topic.

Internships/College Work Experience

Like post-college work, most schools do not have specific requirements for the types of internships or college work experiences that applicants should have. What's important when choosing your internships or jobs is to find jobs that are intrinsically appealing to you. Since you have four years of college during which you can work, you have the time and opportunity to get many different kinds of experiences and not to limit yourself to one particular area. College should be a time of exploration.

You have much flexibility with regard to working while you are in college, since you have four summers that you can work and you can also work during the school year while you are taking classes. Some students will choose to have the same job throughout college, perhaps returning to the same employer each summer. While this doesn't show any breadth of experience, it shows that you are dependable and reliable and that you are a good worker (or else you wouldn't be hired back every summer). It is particularly helpful for your admissions applications if you can show that you assumed additional responsibility each summer while you worked.

If you choose not to work during your summers, you should be prepared to talk about what you did with your time. While admissions committees don't expect students to work every summer of their college careers, they usually expect that students will work for two or three of those summers. Even if you don't need to work for the money, you should be doing something worthwhile with your time during the summer, which could include taking an unpaid internship or volunteering.

You also can work during the school year. Some people will have to work in order to support themselves through school. Even if you don't have to work for the money, working is one way to show that you are disciplined and motivated. It's also a way to have experiences that you might not be exposed to otherwise.

Whether you are looking for a summer job or for term-time work, working for a professor can be beneficial. Even if the work is of a clerical nature, your work can help that professor get to know you better and be able to write a better letter of recommendation for you. If you are thinking about getting a PhD, doing research for a professor can give you an early taste of how well you like that aspect of the profession.

Jerry, a political science major who wanted to go to law school, had an interest in science and was taking a number of science courses. During his sophomore year, he found a position working in a lab with a science professor. He enjoyed the experience so much that he decided to change his plans from law school to medical school.

Being a resident assistant in a residence hall is a good way to develop your people skills that are important in most graduate and professional programs. Other jobs that require you to deal with different kinds of people will help to demonstrate your interpersonal skills to an admissions committee.

As with post-college work experiences, finding college jobs that emphasize writing will be a plus for most admissions committees. Not only will you hone your writing skills, but you will give the person you are writing for another opportunity to evaluate your writing and be able to comment on it in a letter of recommendation.

If you choose not to work during the academic year, you need to spend your time doing something besides studying, especially if you want to become a well-rounded person (the kind of person admissions committees like to see). The next section will talk about the role of extracurricular activities in the admissions process and whether particular types of activities are more valuable than others.

Extracurricular Activities

Some students spend most of their free time in college getting involved in every conceivable type of activity offered at the school. Others spend their time engaging in intellectual conversations with classmates and being more contemplative. Still others might spend all their time studying, while others will just have fun. How are all of these people evaluated when they apply to graduate or professional school? Are admissions committees looking for certain types of activities? Do they prefer breadth or depth? This section will answer those questions and explore the role of extracurricular activities in the admissions process.

Evaluating extracurricular activities can be a bit tricky, because your involvement with an activity might not be the same as your roommate's involvement with the same activity. Simply seeing, "Member, Biology Club, 1997–1998" doesn't tell the admissions committee much about what you did as a member of the biology club. Perhaps you organized the club's annual conference, and that took 10 hours a week for the first semester of the year. Perhaps you simply attended meetings when you felt like it, which averaged about once a month. If you don't tell an admissions committee what you did, there is no way for them to know it.

There is a fine line, though, between describing in detail every extracurricular activity in which you were involved and giving a brief synopsis of the most significant activities. The way you deal with this issue is very telling regarding your judgment and your ability to distinguish what's important from what's insignificant.

Patti submitted a one-page standard résumé with her application and she also submitted an addendum that expanded upon the items on her résumé. This addendum was five pages long and contained a paragraph description of everything she had done in college. The committee was not interested in wading through this voluminous material. Peter submitted a two-page résumé that included a bit more detail than a standard résumé but gave the committee more useful information about what he had actually done. He omitted a number of insignificant activities from the résumé and used one or two sentences to highlight items such as the "Bones Memorial Prize," which by itself didn't seem important, but gained great significance with his explanation that it was the top prize awarded to one chemistry student every year.

Showing passion for something by getting involved in one area in great depth can be very appealing to an admissions committee. It shows that you have the ability to focus and immerse yourself. If your interests are a bit more eclectic and you have been involved in a number of activities, that can also work to your advantage if you can show that you made significant contributions to some of those activities and that you weren't just looking to pad your résumé or have superficial involvement in a number of areas.

Being successful as a varsity athlete tells an admissions committee a great deal about your motivation, drive, and determination, some of the qualities that were discussed in Chapter 5 on the admissions process. A successful scholar-athlete demonstrates the ability to prioritize and manage time. If you played a team sport, you learned about the value of teamwork and being able to get along with others. Some admissions committees may give varsity athletes a slight break on their GPAs, since they recognize that athletics requires an enormous time commitment, although no amount of success on the athletic field can make up for terrible grades.

Significant leadership experiences are also important to admissions committees. You can demonstrate leadership by being elected president of an existing college organization, or you can take the initiative and start a new organization. Both types of leadership are recognized. In examining your record, admissions committees are looking for evidence that you accomplished something in your leadership positions, not just that you were elected or appointed to serve in leadership roles.

Intramural sports are commonly listed on applications. They are usually viewed as recreational more than substantive. Thus, they tend not to add much to your application. The same can be true for membership in sororities and fraternities, unless you held a significant leadership position within the organization and accomplished something tangible during that time.

Pick and choose wisely where you spend your extra time in college. Select at least a few activities that are related to what you want to study and that will allow you to get involved in more than a perfunctory way.

Graduate School

The first thing to remember in thinking about the role of extracurricular activities in the admissions process is that graduate school is primarily an intellectual endeavor. Therefore, graduate school admissions committees are less interested in the standard sort of extracurricular activities that other programs may be seeking. They are instead looking for evidence of intellectual achievement, which is shown by papers that have been presented, publications, or awards. They will also be interested in whether you belong to any professional associations or have done any type of volunteer or paid work that is related to the field you wish to study.

Graduate schools usually want to see that you have focused yourself in your choice of out-of-class experiences and that the focus is related to the field you want to study. The more you can show that you are serious about your intended field, the better off you will be. Graduate schools prefer depth to breadth.

Medical School

Medical schools like to see that you have had some exposure to the medical profession before entering medical school. This can happen as a volunteer or through work experience at a hospital or clinic. Some hospitals offer premedical observation programs, where students will rotate through different departments as a group, so they can see first-hand what the work is like. They may also hear lectures from doctors as part of this experience. You can check with your pre-medical adviser and with local hospitals to find out if any programs of this nature are offered in your area. You may be able to find a program that you can take advantage of during the summer.

Law School

Some schools have extensive judicial proceedings that deal with student infractions of the honor code or other rules. Students may participate as prosecutors or as a member of the body that determines whether there has been a violation and what the penalty should be. If you have the chance to be significantly involved in this type of process, it may be a positive factor when you are applying to law school. Other activities that might enhance your admission to law school are debate and mock trial. Law schools are not interested in the fact that you shadowed a lawyer for a day or you served as a witness in a law school's mock trial competition.

Community service can be seen as an aspect of extracurricular activities, but many schools view it differently and give it special weight in the admissions process. The next section talks about how community service might be a factor in your application.

Community Service

Community service is similar to extracurricular activities in the role that it plays in the admissions process. It's not required and won't necessarily hurt your application if you don't have any, but it can help your application if you do have some. Most schools are looking for students who are going to be good citizens while they are enrolled and after they have graduated, and if you have shown a propensity for doing community service while you are in college, the likelihood is good that you will continue that involvement throughout your lifetime.

If you are applying to programs that emphasize service to the community, like social work programs, law schools that have strong public interest programs, or medical schools that primarily train students to serve underrepresented communities, your community service record will be of particular importance. Schools with those types of programs are looking for students with strong, sustained records of community service.

When considering community service activities, schools are looking for more than working in a soup kitchen once a year with an organization to which you belong. Although you don't have to spend every other day at a soup kitchen to demonstrate a commitment to community service, it looks rather transparent when applicants list on their résumés community service activities that are clearly sporadic in nature.

Serena's résumé, which she submitted with her application, had a section labeled "Community Service." Under that heading, she listed: 1991–92— Donated food and clothing to a drive being held at school. 1992–93— Sang Christmas carols at the nursing home. 1993–94— Spent a day cleaning up a local park. 1994–95— Spent two evenings helping at the homeless shelter. Compare Serena's experience with Rashad, who wrote that from 1992–93, he spent a significant amount of time organizing a charity dance to raise money to fight multiple sclerosis. Although Rashad only had one year of community service activity on his résumé, his sustained effort at a project that was clearly important to him was more impressive than Serena's four years of very minor community service activities.

Writing Experience

Since writing will be a major component of many graduate and professional school programs, any writing that you have done prior to admission will be important. An obvious source of writing is the undergraduate courses you have taken, but you can also seek out other opportunities to demonstrate your writing skills, either through writing for the school newspaper, writing a scholarly article and submitting it to a journal, or having a poem or short story published.

Depending on the program to which you are applying, editing experience can also be a positive factor in the admissions process. Editing experience typically can be found through newspapers or college journals.

Getting to Know Your Adviser

An adviser can be of great assistance to you as you prepare your applications for graduate or professional school. Unfortunately, the quality of advisers varies greatly from school to school, so you may have to search a bit to find one who will work best for you. You may find that the school-designated adviser isn't particularly helpful in your situation, so you may need to seek out someone else who knows about the programs to which you are applying and who can give you sound advice about how to proceed. The role of advisers varies a bit from program to program, so we'll cover each type of program separately.

Law School

A very large number of colleges and universities have designated pre-law advisers. These advisers may have advising as their full-time job or they may be faculty members who have agreed to serve as a central source of information for pre-law students. They may also be academic or administrative deans who have pre-law advising as one of their duties or they may be a counselor in the career services office. You will find great variations in pre-law advisers' interest in and commitment to their advisees.

The best pre-law advisers will have contacts at a number of law schools and will be able to help you realistically assess where you can be admitted based on your background. They can also give you advice about how to prepare for the LSAT, how to write your personal statement, and what kind of information to include in your application. Some pre-law advisers will even call a school to find out your chances of admission before you apply or to find out the status of your application after you have applied.

You may find that some pre-law advisers will simply tell you where you can get information and will be able to give you general advice and information about the law school admissions process, but won't be able to tell you anything specific about individual schools.

Regardless of the reputation of the pre-law adviser at your undergraduate school, you owe it to yourself to find out who that person is and to get in touch with him or her as early as possible in the admissions process. If you meet with the adviser and decide that she or he can't meet your needs in the way you would like, you can ask some of your professors if they know anything about the law school admissions process or if there is anyone else on campus who acts as an informal adviser to students wanting to go to law school.

Medical School

If you are applying to medical school, chances are good that your undergraduate school will have a pre-medical adviser. If a large percentage of students from your college go on to medical school, your college may have even established a pre-medical council, which is essentially a group version of a pre-medical adviser. What was said in the previous section about pre-law advisers applies as well to pre-medical advisers. The major difference is that medical schools require a recommendation letter from your pre-medical adviser. This person may even write a committee recommendation letter for you that will include information from many sources.

Graduate and Business School

Colleges generally do not have advisers designated for graduate school or business school. The reason is that most people who are going to apply to business school will do so after they have been out of school for a few years, so colleges don't see a need to have an adviser on campus. With respect to graduate school, since there are so many different graduate programs and usually not a large number of students applying to any particular graduate program in any year, it doesn't make sense to have a graduate school adviser. Instead, colleges rely on their professors to serve as advisers to students who wish to enter graduate school.

Your professors all attended graduate school, so they know about the process from their own experiences. If you attend a university that has a graduate school, some of your professors are probably involved in the graduate school admissions process, so they know how it works there. If you want an adviser to help you through the graduate school admissions process, you will have to seek out a professor in that subject who will be willing to spend time talking with you about admissions requirements and different schools.

Conclusion

As you have seen, there is no prescription for what you have to do to be admitted to the schools of your choice. Many different types of preparation will work, and you can choose many kinds of activities that will help you develop as a person and that will be looked upon favorably in the admissions process. The key factor is to make thoughtful choices and consider whether a particular activity will advance your mission of being admitted to a graduate or professional school program.

Section 3
Making It Happen

chapter 7

The Graduate and Professional School Experience

Before you enter into the endeavor of graduate or professional school, it could help for you to understand what your schooling will be like. This chapter will tell you what you can expect once you enroll, so you will be able to approach your studies with the right attitude.

Stress

A realistic attitude assumes that you will feel stress during your graduate and professional studies. Some people will experience minor stress, while others will have major stress. Your reaction to graduate or professional school will probably be similar to your reactions to other stressful situations in your life. If you can determine what causes you stress, you might be able to manage it better. It is also helpful to know some general ways to avoid stress during school.

Being able to recognize and manage your stress will be key to your success in graduate and professional school.

The most important thing you can do to avoid stress is not to let your studies consume your life. It is easy to allow that to happen, but with a little work, you can make sure to include other things in your life as well. You may not be able to spend as much time going to the movies, reading for pleasure, or listening to music as you did in the past, but you should arrange your schedule in such a way that it includes some time every week for activities you enjoy that are unrelated to school. Thus, being in an extracurricular activity at school doesn't count.

If you exercise regularly, you should definitely find time to keep doing that. If you don't exercise much, you might consider working it into your schedule while you are in graduate or professional school. Exercise is a great stress-reliever, will give you more energy, and will help you sleep better at night. One good way to build exercise into your schedule is to see if you can audit or enroll in a physical education class at your university. You can also take advantage of the gyms, pools, and other athletic facilities available at your university. These facilities are usually free or available for a nominal charge.

When Amanda began graduate school, she knew she needed to find a way to exercise regularly. She looked into the physical education course offerings at her university and found that they offered a class in Aikido, a Japanese martial art. She had been wanting to try something new, so she signed up. Two years later she was still taking Aikido and found it to a wonderful way to unwind.

Eating well is another way to help avoid stress. If you drink too much caffeine and don't eat enough fruits and vegetables, your body will rebel. It's easy to get caught in the fast food or junk food trap because it's quick and it's convenient, but there are ways to eat a balanced diet. You may even find that cooking is a relaxing pasttime for you and will take your mind off of school for a period of time every day.

Don't short-change your sleep. You might think that you can survive on four hours of sleep a night, but it will catch up with you. Studies have shown that people who get less than eight hours of sleep a night are not as mentally sharp as they are when they get eight hours or more of sleep, even if the people don't think that they are suffering any impairment.

The last way to alleviate stress is to try to learn quickly what is most important in your discipline and what can be ignored. You will be given a vast amount of material to study and learn, but it is not all equally important. Part of your schooling is learning how to discern the significant from the trivial.

Socializing

In addition to expecting stress in graduate and professional school, you should expect that you will be making professional acquaintances and friendships that will stay with you throughout your career. Focusing on the social aspects of school is good and will allow you to form relationships that can be important to you during school and for years beyond. Getting to know faculty members as well as fellow students is important, as your professors can act as mentors for many years.

Randy attended a reception for alumni of his MBA program. He had been out of the program for 20 years, and he said the one thing he regretted is that he didn't take the time to get to know his classmates very well during the program. He was married while in school and felt like he didn't have enough time for his studies, his wife, and his classmates, so he didn't spend much time with the classmates. As time passed, he realized how crucial those contacts could have been, so 20 years later he was trying to reconnect with people with whom he had gone to school.

Depending on your program, it may be quite easy to develop a deep relationship with your classmates. If you're in a graduate program that only enrolls ten students, it will be hard for you not to get to know the other nine. That's why when you are selecting a program that has a small enrollment, you should pay close attention to the students who are currently in the program to make sure that you will have something in common with them. If you enroll in a larger program, you may have to work a little harder to meet people, but you will have more students to choose from as you try to find people with similar values and interests.

Medical School

The major difference between undergraduate school and medical school is the level of competition that you will face with your fellow classmates (after all, they have all graduated at the top of their classes and have received a high score on the MCAT). The competition is more apparent because you are all taking the same courses, so it is easy to compare yourself to others. You will also find that the first two years of medical school are very fact-oriented and that you will be required to memorize a huge amount of material. Most medical students can be found hunched over their books memorizing, memorizing, memorizing.

Students who come to medical school from small colleges are often dismayed to discover how impersonal medical school is. Courses are taught by multiple instructors, so there is no real opportunity to establish a relationship with a faculty member. Also hindering the ability to develop relationships with professors is the fact that classes are taught in large lecture formats. Some schools even videotape these lectures, so students who are unable or choose not to attend class can check out the videotape and watch the lecture at their leisure.

During the first year of medical school, students spend about 35 hours per week split equally between lectures and labs. The three classes that most medical schools require students to take during this year are physiology, anatomy, and biochemistry, all of the elements of normal human biology. The thought is that students need to learn how the body normally functions before they can learn about how it can function improperly. Other courses you might take are embrology, histology, behavioral science, genetics, and ethics.

> Jennifer's gross anatomy class was taught by having students work in teams dissecting cadavers for the entire semester. She found that it was a great way to learn the human body, since she was able to see all of its parts and not just read about them in a book.

The second year is devoted to the study of abnormal human biology. You will study subjects like microbiology, pharmacology, pathology, physical diagnosis, and clinical lab procedures. You may also be exposed to some specialty fields like psychiatry. Lectures and labs will continue during your second year and will be supplemented by clinical pathology conferences.

After the second year of medical school, you must pass Part 1 of the United States Medical Licensing Examination (USMLE). If you do not pass, you will probably not be allowed to continue in medical school. Many hospitals will consider your score on this test when they are deciding whether to offer you a residency. Before you can be licensed to practice medicine, you will have to pass Parts 2 and 3 of this exam.

During the third year you will have two-month rotations in different areas. It is common for schools to require rotations in surgery, obstetrics/gynecology, internal medicine, pediatrics, and psychiatry. Some schools may only require four rotations, and some schools may let you have an elective rotation during the year. In addition to working with patients, you will be expected to attend some lectures and conferences during your rotation, and you will have to study on your own, so you can be sure you understand the nuances of the area in which you are rotating. You will have an exam at the end of each rotation, and you will be on call every three to four nights. The emphasis this year will be on teaching you how to diagnosis disease. Since you will be acting more as a doctor would during this year, your relationship with your professors will become closer than during the first two years.

Your fourth year will consist entirely of electives, and you will continue the rotations of the third year. You may choose to spend more rotations in areas you experienced during your third year or you may choose some other areas. This is the year when you will interview for your residency and go through the residency match program. Near the end of this year, you will take Part 2 of the United States Medical Licensing Examination, which will cover pediatrics, psychiatry, internal medicine, obstetrics/gynecology, and surgery. Some schools require passage of Part 2 in order to graduate.

Law School

The common saying for law school is that during the first year, they will scare you to death, during the second year, they will work you to death, and during the third year, they will bore you to death. There is some truth to that saying.

Your first year of law school may be intimidating because the professors use something called the Socratic method to teach. The Socratic method is a way of asking questions that build upon each other and leading you, the student who is answering the questions, to a conclusion that may be unsupported. The idea is to teach you and show you in a graphic way the importance of thinking logically and anticipating how an answer to one question can lead you to an undesirable result.

You may be surprised to find that the nightly reading assignments are comparatively short, especially if you were an English major and are used to reading hundreds of pages a week. However, while they are short, they are difficult, because you have to read and understand terms that you have never heard before. Most law students' first purchase is a law dictionary, which they refer to constantly while doing their readings.

In addition to the Socratic method, law schools use the case method. They assign students to read court opinions that have been written in real cases. Students are then expected to derive the underlying legal principles from those opinions. The case method is used throughout all three years of school, although the Socratic method is usually more prevalent during the first year.

In most classes, especially during the first year, your grades will be based on one examination given at the end of the semester. The exam will present a long, involved situation and ask you to identify any possible legal issues in that situation, and then discuss how you would resolve those issues. What is being tested is not your ability to memorize legal rules but your ability to analyze a fact pattern and apply legal rules to that fact pattern.

During your first year of law school, your class will be divided into sections and will be assigned to a required set of courses. You will have all of your courses with your section, so you will get to know those students quite well. Although there will be some variations from school to school, the basic curriculum consists of Torts, Contracts, Property, Criminal Law, Constitutional Law, Civil Procedure, and Legal Research and Writing. The concepts you learn in these courses will serve as building blocks for later courses. The first year is when you learn legal vocabulary, the proper way to read and analyze cases, and how to write like a lawyer. Even though you may be an excellent writer, you will find that legal writing is in a class by itself.

Many students will spend a week or two getting to know their classmates before asking them to join a study group. Study groups may have anywhere from four to eight students who meet together throughout the semester to study together. They also work together to write outlines of the courses that they will use to study for their final examinations.

At most law schools, your second and third years consist of elective courses, except for one required course in Professional Responsibility. Courses that are most commonly selected by students in these years are Administrative Law, Corporations, Estates and Trusts, and Commercial Paper. These are usually large courses that are taught in a similar manner to your first year courses. You can also choose from esoteric topics like Icelandic Blood Feuds and Maritime Law. Students enjoy the opportunity to take seminars during these years (usually no more than one per semester), where they will be enrolled in small classes and will take turns leading class discussions each week.

You may feel like you are worked to death during your second year, because in addition to your regular load of courses, you may be working on the law review at your school or competing in a moot court competition. Second year is the most active year of student involvement during law school.

At the beginning of the second semester of law school, Cindy had the opportunity to sign up for the moot court competition. She was a bit nervous, especially since she didn't know anyone she could ask to be her partner, but she signed up anyway. The moot court board assigned another second-year student to her as a partner and they became a team. They were given a made-up legal case that had already been decided by a lower court and told that they had to represent one side in the dispute when the case went before the Supreme Court. They had to research the legal issues and then write a 30-page brief outlining their position. They went on to argue the case in front of mock judges. Cindy and her partner did so well that they ended up being semifinalists in the school-wide competition. During the course of the competition, she became adept at speaking on her feet and answering questions she hadn't previously anticipated.

Most students spend a good deal of their time in the second year looking for summer jobs. Large law firms start their hiring process in September for positions for the following summer. If you attend a school that has an on-campus interview program, you will begin interviewing shortly after you return to classes in the fall. You will then go on callback interviews at the law firms during your first semester. The majority of large law firms have completed their hiring by the first of December. These summer jobs are important if you want to work at a large law firm, because the firms will make offers for employment after graduation based on your performance during the summer.

If you are looking for a job with a government agency, a public interest organization, or a small law firm, your job search probably will not start until the second semester of your second year. Although you will still be seeking a summer job, many of these employers do not make offers of employment to their summer law clerks, so you will have to look for another job during your third year.

You may feel bored during your third year because you have already learned the crucial ability to think like a lawyer, and during your second year, you had the opportunity to take some specialized courses. You will probably have worked during the summer after your second year and performed tasks that are quite similar to what you will be doing after graduation. If you received an offer from your summer employer, you know where you will be working and are eager to get started.

You can alleviate the third-year blues by getting involved in different aspects of the law school. You can be an editor of the law review, be active in a student organization, work part-time, or do pro bono legal work in the community.

Stan spent his last year of law school volunteering as a Guardian Ad Litem and representing a child whose parents had been accused of abuse. He found the experience to be personally rewarding and he learned a lot about how the court system works.

As in medical school, you may feel very intimidated by your classmates because they are high achievers and you will easily be able to compare yourself to others in your section since they will be taking all of the same classes you are taking. Law students also tend to be competitive and argumentative, two traits that may have led them to law school in the first place. Unfortunately, in many university offices that deal with students from across the campus, law students have the worst reputation.

Graduate School

A major difference between graduate school and undergraduate school is the fact that in graduate school, your focus will be narrowed to one specific discipline. You will learn not only the substantive aspects of that discipline but will also learn the important theories and research methods used in it. You will become immersed in your field and will generally not have the opportunity to take classes outside of your discipline. You will spend a lot of time doing research and reading on your own, since you will probably take only two to three courses per semester that will meet only once or twice a week, and you won't have many exams. Your grade for most of your courses will be based on a paper you write for each class.

The next section covers in detail what you can expect if you enroll in a doctorate program.

Doctorate

During your first year, you may be surprised to find yourself taking classes with undergraduate students. Many schools allow undergraduates to take graduate-level courses. Thus, you may find yourself in classes of 100 students, and the teaching method will be lecturing. The first year is an important time for you to get to know your professors and to start thinking about which ones you will want to work with closely in the coming years. If you did not major in the field you are enrolled in for graduate school, you may have to take specific courses that are designed to teach you about major authors or works that you will be expected to know and about theoretical approaches to that discipline.

You will probably take a seminar that will enroll fewer than 15 students. Each student will be responsible for teaching one class during the semester and will have to respond to an assigned reading or present a paper. You will write a final paper for each course. At the end of the first year, you may be asked to take some type of comprehensive exam, pass a foreign language proficiency test, take a required course in pedagogy, or write a paper. Some schools use the first year to determine who is qualified to remain in the program beyond that time. Only the best students will be allowed to continue.

By the end of your first year, you will select an adviser who will remain with you throughout your doctoral program. This person's role is critical in helping you navigate through the program. He or she can help you select your dissertation topic and committee, give you job leads, and hire you to do research.

During your second year, you will begin to be more involved in the process of producing research, possibly by helping faculty work on their research. It is a good idea at this point to try to work with a variety of faculty members, including both those who are more junior and those who are more senior. Junior faculty members may be more aware of new and emerging areas in your discipline, but the senior faculty members are the ones who actually control the department and who can have a great influence on whether you receive your degree. The second year is the time when you begin thinking about the specialty you want to pursue. You will continue taking classes during this year.

You will decide who you want to serve on the committees that will conduct your oral comprehensive exams and direct your dissertation during your third year. This can be a delicate process, as you need to find between five and seven faculty members who will work well together and won't derail your research by in-fighting, but who have different ideas that will prove fertile while you are doing your research. Your committee members should be a source of wisdom and inspiration for you.

You will also spend this year writing a thesis and/or preparing for your oral comprehensive exams (orals), which are a required part of your doctorate program. They are a way to allow you to begin focusing your research and to do an in-depth review of the literature and research available in your discipline. Orals happen at the end of your third year. You may have to take a written exam before you take your orals, or you may just take your orals. Orals can last for as long as two to three days, although they usually last just for a morning or afternoon. The oral exams at some schools are used as a way to assess your academic merit and to determine whether you should continue in the program. At other schools, orals are perfunctory and there is little need to worry about passing them.

Keep your oral exams in perspective. There are legions of stories about students who study like maniacs for their orals and completely stress out about them. Take them seriously, but don't abandon your life while you are preparing for them. Remember that no one expects you to know every arcane detail about a subject. If you find out that everyone passes their oral exams in your program, you can relax even more about them.

Your fourth and subsequent years will be spent researching and writing your dissertation. These are the years when you spend a great deal of time alone in the library or in a lab. It may take you anywhere from five to seven years to write your dissertation, although some students do it in less time and others spend more time. Some people never finish their dissertations and are referred to as *ABD* (all but the dissertation).

Take special care with your research and drafts of your dissertation. Back up your documents frequently on your computer, and consider making a photocopy of particularly important research that it would be difficult to duplicate if it was lost or stolen.

A dissertation typically runs from 100 to 500 pages and is bound in book form. Some dissertations are even published. Your dissertation should summarize existing research but should add a new twist to it so that it is unique and conveys something that hasn't been said before. Your dissertation will be an important document when you try to get a teaching job. The recommendations you receive from members of your dissertation committee will also be important. Unless you are one of the fortunate few who receives a grant, fellowship, or some other type of financial aid, you will probably be working during the years that you are writing your dissertation. It requires a great deal of discipline and dedication to work and complete a dissertation, so careful planning for this stage of the process is important.

The key to finishing your dissertation in a reasonable amount of time is good planning, self-discipline, motivation, and hard work.

Once you complete your dissertation, you will be asked to *defend* it, which means to appear before your dissertation committee and answer questions about it. This can be another anxiety-producing time in your life, since your performance on your defense will determine whether you earn your PhD. The good news is that once you have defended successfully, you will have earned your doctorate.

Before you are allowed to graduate, you may have to demonstrate your proficiency in a foreign language. Over the years, there has been much controversy over foreign language requirements, so they are far less common than they used to be. Requirements vary greatly from department to department. Some departments expect you to know three languages, while others require only one. You may have to be able to speak, read, and write proficiently in another language, or you may only need to know how to read that language. Depending on your department and your language proficiency before entering the program, you may need to find time in your schedule to learn or brush up your language skills.

Master's Degree

Like all other graduate and professional degree programs, master's degree programs are challenging. Part of the challenge comes from the fact that you probably aren't receiving much in the way of financial aid, so you are working to reduce the amount of money you have to borrow to finance your education. Although it may add to the stress of graduate school, this is a particularly smart strategy if you plan to enter one of the traditionally lower-paid professions like education or social work.

Most master's degree programs require their students to maintain a B average. Consequently, most grades awarded in master's programs tend to be As or Bs. It is rare for a graduate student to receive a C, and if you do, you might ask yourself whether you should be enrolled in that program.

There are two types of master's degree programs: the terminal master's and the master's that you receive after completing two years of a PhD program.

The terminal master's degree is usually awarded in programs such as social work, education, computer science, or engineering that prepare you to enter a specific profession. In this type of program, you will take the courses required by your school plus electives. You may decide to specialize in a particular area that will dictate the types of electives you may wish to choose. Some programs will require you to do fieldwork as part of your degree, which could last for one or two semesters of your two-year program.

If you are enrolled in a master's degree program that leads to a PhD, your first two years will be the equivalent of the first two years of a PhD program. Some schools will award a master's degree when you have completed a certain number of requirements; others will not give you a degree even if you have finished two years of the program and decide that you no longer wish to pursue your PhD, or you are told by your department that you can no longer pursue a PhD.

Celeste entered a PhD program in English, but after two years, she decided that she didn't want to continue. Her school awarded her a master's degree to recognize her work during that two-year period.

Some master's degree programs will require you to write a thesis that will demonstrate your ability to do in-depth research on a specialized subject. Theses range in length from 50 to 250 pages, although the average length is 100 pages. Although you will not receive your degree until you have completed your thesis, you are usually not required to finish the thesis during your two years in the program. This means that your thesis writing can continue past the point when you have finished your course work or your fieldwork. Dragging out the writing process in that way is clearly not a good idea.

Failing to complete your thesis in a timely manner will delay the receipt of your degree. It may also irritate your adviser, and you may run out of time if the school requires you to complete your degree requirements within a specified amount of time.

Prior to receiving your master's degree, you may have to demonstrate your mastery of a foreign language. This requirement has become less common than it used to be, but it still exists in about 20 percent of graduate schools. A foreign language requirement would be more common in a field such as international relations and less common for a field such as computer science. Departments typically are more concerned with your reading ability than your speaking ability, since you will have to be able to read a foreign language to conduct research in that language. The most common languages departments require are German, Russian, and French.

Business School

If you pursue a full-time MBA program, it will take you two years to earn your degree. Business schools vary in their core course requirements, although most will require accounting (often managerial and financial), marketing, finance, economics (macroeconomics and microeconomics may be combined in one course, or you may have to take two separate courses), information systems, operations, business policy/strategy, organizational behavior, and statistics or quantitative methods. You may find that your entire first year consists of required courses, and you won't have any electives until your second year, or you may have many electives during both years.

If you have already worked in a particular subject matter area or you have a strong familiarity with the subject, you may be able to exempt some of the required courses. However, some schools may still require you to take that subject, because they think that you will add a great deal of real-world experience to the class.

Hans was a whiz at finance because of his years of working in that industry. When his finance class discussed leveraged buyouts, he was able to share with his classmates details of a recent leveraged buyout on which he had worked. The class understood the concept better from having heard about it from someone who had worked in that area.

Although the case method is talked about frequently in connection with business schools, there are only a handful of schools that use it as their primary method of teaching. Other schools may use it for some of their classes but not for a majority of them. The case method in business school is quite different from the case method in law school. In business school, the case you study may be made-up or based on a real situation and will involve a business problem. You will have to analyze the case and determine the best action to take. Cases may be quite complex and involve large amounts of material that must be read and digested.

The most common teaching method in business school is lectures. Lecturing in business school is the same as lecturing in other programs. The professor stands at the lectern and speaks, and you take notes.

You may attend a school where one or more courses will be taught using computer simulation. In this type of learning, you will be given a situation similar to that which you might receive as part of a case study. The difference is that the actions you decide the company should take will be fed into a computer, along with the actions that every other course member has decided his or her company should take. The computer will analyze all of these actions to determine what actually happens to the industry.

Business schools encourage students to form study groups to help them through business school. A school may even assign you to a study group. Assignments will usually be made to maximize the number of different backgrounds to insure that the group as a whole is strong in a variety of business skills. If you are not assigned to a study group, it is wise to choose your study group carefully and to try to find people who have strengths in areas where you are weaker. Your study group can help you prepare during the semester and for final exams, or you might be assigned group projects with your study group.

Samantha was assigned to a study group when she arrived at business school. When she had to make a presentation to the class, she used her study group to practice beforehand. When she was sick or out interviewing, members of her study group allowed her to copy their notes. When it came time for exams, they studied together extensively to make sure they all understood the material.

During your first year of business school, you will be participating in on-campus interviews and seeking a summer job. As with law school, if you do well during the summer, you will probably be made an offer to return to work after graduation. Thus, the first-year job search is quite important.

Like medical schools, business schools will give you a vast amount of material to study. The difference is that in medical school, you are expected to memorize it and be able to regurgitate it on exams. In business school, you are expected to be able to determine what is essential from what is non-essential and concentrate only on the essential. Business schools are trying to simulate a world where there will be many demands placed on your time and it will be impossible to meet all of those demands. Thus, it is expected that you won't be able to do all of the work, but it will be up to you to decide what not to do.

Conclusion

As is obvious from this chapter, you will not have much time to sit back and relax while you are in graduate or professional school. In fact, you will probably have to work to find time for yourself, your friends, and your family. Graduate and professional school is an intense time that allows you to pursue a field in great depth. It can be quite exhilarating to be surrounded by so many other intelligent people who are all hungry for knowledge and eager to talk about the same concepts that excite you. You will probably never again experience as much intellectual challenge as you will have during the next two to ten years of your life. Enjoy, and make the most of it!

Financial Aid

Now that you have become deeply invested in your plans to go to graduate or professional school, you may be worried about how to pay for it. You're right to be concerned, as financing your graduate or professional school education will be a major investment. You may think that there's no way you can afford to pursue an advanced degree because neither you nor your parents are wealthy. This chapter will tell you about the many sources of financial aid available for graduate and professional school and will also help you learn how to deal with the apparent maze of financial aid. Two worksheets are included at the end of the chapter to help you calculate your income and expenses for each school you are considering. As you will see, it is possible to pay for your education, regardless of your income level, as long as you are willing to borrow money and you do not have credit problems.

The cost of a law degree can exceed $100,000, medical school can cost as much as $200,000, and business school costs can exceed $80,000. Although it can be easy to feel overwhelmed by the cost of attending graduate or professional school, keep in mind that you are investing in your future. The U.S. Census Bureau shows that those who have a professional degree can expect lifetime earnings of $3 million, while the lifetime earnings of those with just a bachelor's degree average only $1.4 million.

Start thinking about financial aid as soon as you start thinking about attending graduate or professional school.

Financial aid consists of all resources other than those you and your family can provide. It is composed of three main sources: free money (grants and scholarships), money from working (assistantships or work-study positions), and loans (both federal and private). It is important to understand all types of aid and to know which type of aid is being offered to you by each school to which you apply. While you might be one of those people whose eyes glaze over when you think about financial aid, it is fairly simple if you learn some basics and if you keep good records.

The first step in obtaining financial aid is to talk to the schools to which you will be applying. Each school should be able to provide you with detailed information about its financial aid policies and procedures. Start with the admissions office, which can tell you how to contact the financial aid office. Some schools have their own financial aid offices, while others use the university's central financial aid office. At some graduate schools, the financial aid process may be handled by the individual academic department. If you have to deal with more than one office in the university regarding your financial aid, it is even more critical to keep good records of what each office has told you and to make sure you understand what each office can and cannot do for you.

When you are talking to the financial aid office, certain questions will help you learn the financial aid process at that school. These questions include:

- What percentage of students receive financial aid?
- Do you guarantee to meet students' demonstrated need? If not, what percentage of their need is met?
- What percentage of students receive loans?
- Does the school have its own loan program? What are the rates?
- Does the school recommend that students use "preferred" lenders? If so, what are those lenders' rates?

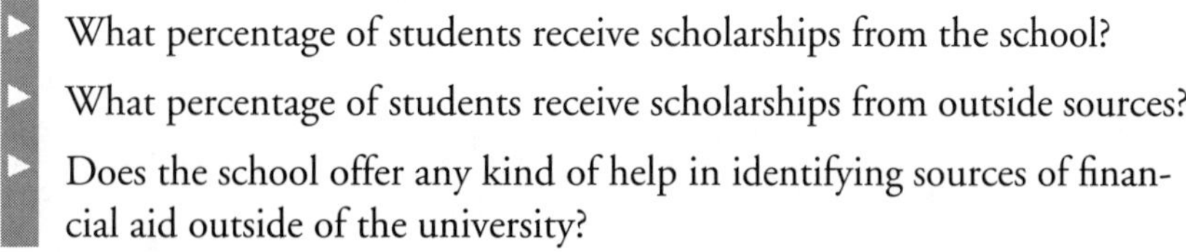

- What percentage of students receive scholarships from the school?
- What percentage of students receive scholarships from outside sources?
- Does the school offer any kind of help in identifying sources of financial aid outside of the university?

You may be thinking that this chapter doesn't apply to you, because as an undergraduate, your parents' income kept you from getting financial aid. Good news! As a graduate or professional student, you will automatically be considered independent of your parents for purposes of determining your eligibility for federal aid. Thus, you can still qualify for those desirable federal loans based only on *your* income and assets, not your parents'.

Some schools may still consider your parents' income and assets when they are considering you for sources of aid that they control, like school grants. The reason for this is that their resources are generally more limited and they want to consider an applicant's entire financial picture when determining how to allocate them.

When determining your eligibility for federal loans, only your income and not your parents' income will be considered.

The rest of this chapter will cover in depth the topics touched on in the previous paragraphs. You will learn about various sources for free money, what kind of work programs might be available, and the types of loans that are offered for graduate and professional students. By the end of the chapter, you will know what kind of financial aid you can get and how to go about finding it.

Scholarships, Grants, and Fellowships

Scholarships, grants, and fellowships are the most desirable form of financial aid, since they are provided free, with no work or repayment requirements. Depending on the program you are pursuing, they may cover the cost of tuition and may also include a stipend to help pay for living costs. Full tuition awards are more typical in graduate school, particularly in PhD programs, than in professional school. Many PhD programs provide full funding for all or almost all of their students. While professional schools may offer a few full tuition awards, they expect the majority of students to pay their own way, or at least a substantial portion of their way. A similar situation exists with respect to master's degree programs, which offer very little funding for their students.

> Some people believe that if they aren't offered full funding to attend a PhD program, the school must not be very interested in them. While this may be true, you should ask the school what level of funding it is providing to other students. If you find that only one student in your department is getting full funding, you will know that the decision not to give you full funding has less to do with your perceived merit at that school than with an institutional decision about how much funding to provide.

Some grants are based solely on financial need, while others are based on merit, and still others are based on a combination of need and merit. Typically, fellowships and scholarships indicate that you were selected based on merit; need may have been a negligible factor. Grants most often are based on need. These terms have become rather interchangeable, though, and it probably doesn't matter what your award is called, as long as you know that the money does not have to be repaid.

PhD students should be aware that it may be more difficult to find free money for the first year of their program and for the years when they are writing their dissertations. If a school offers you a seemingly generous financial aid package, find out just how generous it is by asking whether it includes money for the years when you will be writing your dissertation. If not, you may find that financing those years will be a bit of a challenge, and you should plan accordingly.

If you really want to access some of the free money that is available for graduate and professional students, be willing to devote time to look for various sources of money. If you are creative, persistent, and willing to fill out some applications, you can often find some free money to help you through school.

The rest of this section will go into detail about the different types of free money available. They are:

- Institutional aid
- Federal support
- State support
- Corporate aid
- Foundation aid
- Other sources

Institutional Aid

The most common source of scholarships, grants, and fellowships is the university you will be attending. Universities award between $2 and $3 billion each year to graduate and professional students. Some scholarships require special applications; others will be granted based upon your application for admission. The best source of information on this type of aid is the school itself, either through printed materials or the Web site.

Don't just rely on the written materials. Contact the financial aid office and ask what process the school uses to award its free money. If there is a special application that needs to be completed, get a copy of it and find out the deadline date. If the funding decision is based on your admissions application, find out if there is any particular information you can include in your application that will increase your chances of getting funding.

Many schools rely on the interest from endowment funds to finance the scholarships they offer. These endowment funds may have been set up with certain restrictions (for example, the recipient must be a resident of the state of Massachusetts), but if the school has a large pool of scholarship money, what usually happens is that the school selects scholarship recipients based on who it most desires to have in the class or who is the neediest. After the offers have been accepted, the school will find someone who has been offered a scholarship who meets the endowment's restrictions and will make sure that the money for that person's scholarship comes from that endowed scholarship.

If a school has a smaller pool of scholarship funds available, it may make decisions at the beginning as to who will be offered which scholarship. In that case, the school may have to find someone who meets the endowment's restrictions and then give the scholarship to that applicant, even if that person is not necessarily the neediest or the most qualified. The school might also decide not to award the scholarship that year.

If you are offered a scholarship, fellowship, or grant from a school, you should ask whether that money is only for your first year of study or whether it is guaranteed for all the years you will be enrolled. Some schools will make guaranteed awards when you first enroll, so you never have to worry about the award changing. A school also might say that your award will remain constant as long as you maintain a certain grade point average.

Other schools will give you an award that is good only for the first year and say that the amount of the award can change in subsequent years. If a school has a policy where the award can change, you should ask pointed questions about how likely it is that the award will change, on what grounds, and by how much. Also ask current students who are on financial aid whether their awards changed from year to year and if so, by how much.

Sarah enrolled at a school that offered her a full tuition award for her first year. Although her award letter said that the award was only for the first year, she overlooked that and was shocked to find out during her second year that she would not receive any money.

Questions you can ask the school regarding scholarships include the following:

- What percentage of students receive scholarships from the school?
- What is the average amount of an individual scholarship at the school?
- What is the lowest scholarship offered? What is the highest?
- What percentage of the scholarships are need-based? What percentage are merit-based?
- Does the average amount of need-based scholarships differ from the average amount of merit-based scholarships?
- When considering applicants for need-based scholarships, does the school consider only the applicant's income and assets or does it also include the applicant's parents' income and assets?

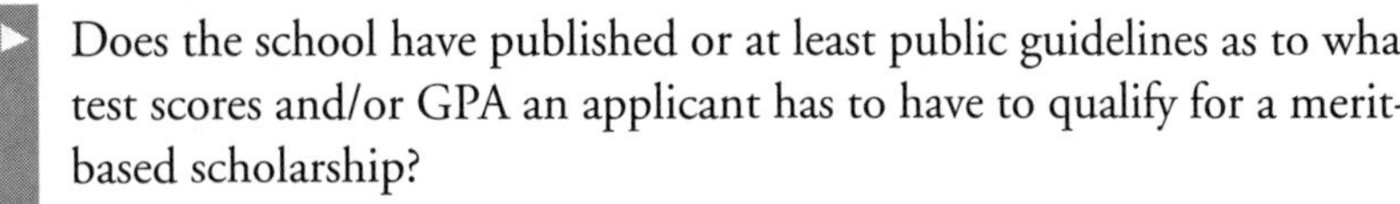

- Does the school have published or at least public guidelines as to what test scores and/or GPA an applicant has to have to qualify for a merit-based scholarship?
- Has the school published its formula for determining need?

Determine and follow the school's deadlines for applying for financial aid.

Federal Support

Although the federal government does not provide Pell grants to graduate or professional students, it does provide other types of support. The amounts and types of assistance offered vary considerably by field of study. The National Health Services Corps Scholarship, provided by the U.S. Public Health Service, pays the entire cost of medical school for students who are willing to commit to working for four years as a primary care physician in an underserved area after earning their MDs.

If you are interested in serving in the military, all four branches of the armed forces also have programs that will pay for medical school. The Armed Forces Health Professions Scholarship provides full tuition, payment of educational expenses, plus a large stipend. Students receiving this aid must serve one year of active military duty for each year of support they receive. The usual minimum length of service is three years.

The armed forces also offer scholarships for law students. If you are currently in the military, you can apply for a scholarship that will pay for your law school in exchange for a certain number of years of active duty after graduation. These scholarships are very competitive. Since application requirements and procedures can vary between the different branches of the armed forces, you should check with each for more information.

State Support

You may find that some states will provide scholarships or other types of financial aid for graduate and professional students. These programs will usually be for residents of that state and will be targeted to achieve some result that the state thinks is worthy. Currently, 13 states offer some type of financial aid, including scholarships, to medical students who agree to practice in the inner city or in remote areas of the state.

Corporate Aid

Some employers will provide tuition benefits to employees who wish to pursue a graduate or professional education. These tuition benefits are more common for people who attend school part-time rather than full-time, although some employers also offer tuition reimbursement for full-time study. If you are currently employed, check with your human resources office for more information. This is also an option for you to explore if you are thinking about working after college and are concerned about the cost of attending graduate or professional school. You may be able to find work with an employer who offers tuition reimbursement if you work for them for a certain number of years.

> John had worked in the engineering department of a company for about 10 years, and he decided he wanted to go to law school so he could practice patent law. The company agreed to pay for all of his tuition if he would go to school part-time and continue working for that company. John preferred to attend a law school out-of-state, so he had to balance his competing needs and desires.

Tuition benefit policies vary from employer to employer, so as with everything else regarding financial aid, you need to ask. Some employers will provide tuition aid only if you are pursuing a degree that will be beneficial to the current job you are doing (sometimes employers can define that rather broadly). Others will provide aid for any type of class. An employer may have an arrangement with a particular school and will only provide tuition benefits if you attend that school. If the company is large enough, it sometimes will make arrangements to have classes taught on-site.

In some cases, the employer will pay your tuition directly to the school. In other cases, you have to pay the tuition, get a passing grade in the course, and then apply for reimbursement of your tuition. Some employers will place a cap on the amount of tuition they will reimburse. Others will reimburse you based on the grade you earn in the course. As an example, they may pay you 100 percent if you earn an A, 75 percent if you get a B, and 50 percent for a C.

Jane worked for a large corporation in Colorado. It had a special program to allow selected people to get their MBAs, which the corporation paid for. Jane attended evening and weekend classes for a few months during the year. She then spent a month each summer taking classes in another state. It took her four years to get her MBA, but the corporation paid for all of it and gave her the paid time off to take the necessary classes.

Foundation Aid

Many foundations provide support to graduate students who are pursuing degrees in areas of interest to the foundation. The National Science Foundation provides generous fellowships for students in the social sciences and the physical sciences. The Foundation Center publishes a book, *Foundation Grants to Individuals*, that can help you identify numerous possibilities. See Chapter 11 for more information.

Other Sources

There are a large number of private organizations that provide scholarships to students. Although money is more plentiful for undergraduates than for graduate or professional students, there is still money available for graduate and professional schools. It takes some time and work to identify appropriate sources of scholarships for your situation, but the free money that can result makes the effort worthwhile. You can check with civic organizations, your parents' employer, and national organizations like the American Association of University Women (AAUW). Many schools will be able to tell you which organizations have provided funding for their students in the past. Chapter 11 also can give you ideas on how to identify potential organizational funding.

Work Programs

Work offered through the university is the second best type of financial aid, because in many cases, you not only receive a salary for your work but your tuition is waived as well. At some schools, students who receive an assistantship may not get a tuition waiver but they may be considered state residents and thus be eligible for in-state tuition rates, which can result in substantial tuition savings.

A general point to keep in mind when thinking about accepting an assistantship is to make sure that the number of hours you are asked to work will not interfere with your studies. Students generally find that working no more than 25 hours per week is best for them. Also note that many departments won't award assistantships to students who are in the first year of their PhD program, because they want to give them time to become adjusted to the program and see how well they will do academically.

There are three types of assistantships that may provide a tuition waiver in addition to a salary. They are teaching assistantships (TAs), research assistantships (RAs), and administrative assistantships. We'll cover each in turn.

Teaching Assistantships

Teaching assistantships are offered to students who wish to help teach an undergraduate course. First priority is typically given to a graduate student who is pursuing a degree in the field that the course is being taught in. However, other graduate or professional students can sometimes get teaching assistantships depending on their undergraduate major and background.

Academic departments control the awarding of TAs, so you must contact every department that interests you. Typically, there is no centralized system for awarding TAs at a university, and the financial aid office generally does not select the recipients of TAs. In some cases, you may be awarded a TA by your department as part of your financial aid package to entice you to attend that school. This is great if it happens because it means you don't have to do the work of finding the TA position.

As a TA, you may conduct small classes, give lectures, grade papers, counsel students, supervise laboratories, and correct class work. Usually you will be required to work between 10 and 20 hours per week. This is invaluable experience for those who are in PhD programs and who intend to enter academia upon graduation.

Research Assistantships

Research assistantships involve helping a faculty member with his or her research. They are similar to TAs in that there is no centralized system for awarding RAs at the university and the financial aid office is not involved in selecting the recipients. You will usually be required to work between 10 and 20 hours per week. The best way to find a research assistantship is to contact a professor directly who is doing the type of work that interests you or to contact the academic department and describe your research interests.

Miguel was attending business school, but he had a strong science background and an interest in that area. He approached a science professor and asked about doing research for him. The professor was looking for someone with Miguel's background and was delighted to hire him.

Administrative Assistantships

Administrative assistantships are less likely than TAs or RAs to offer a tuition waiver. Like the other positions, they typically require 10 to 20 hours per week of work. Administrative assistants work in an administrative office of the university; duties can vary widely. You can find an administrative assistantship by speaking to your academic department or by approaching university administrative offices directly.

An administrative assistantship is generally considered less enticing than a TA or RA, and you will generally have less autonomy, because you will be working in an office where you will be expected to keep set hours and where someone will be supervising your work more closely. Many offices hire students to work during the school year—the career services office, the admissions office, the dean's office, and the office of minority student affairs, to name only a few. When you are looking for work of this nature, be sure to ask whether it is an assistantship that will pay you a salary and waive your tuition or whether it is an hourly job that pays a relatively low wage.

Lauren found that the dean of students at her school was going to spend a year as president of a national association. The dean was going to need some help with her work at the school during that time but wasn't quite sure how she was going to handle it. Lauren offered to work 10 hours a week for her. The dean found out that by hiring Lauren and paying her $300.00 per month, Lauren's tuition would be waived by the university. Lauren got some exposure to administration and was able to work on interesting admissions marketing strategies and employer outreach programs.

Federal Work Study (FWS)

If you had a Federal Work Study (FWS) position as an undergraduate, you are familiar with how this program works. The federal government provides money to universities to use for employment of students. Most universities favor undergraduates when allocating FWS money, and some only provide money to undergraduate students and do not provide any to graduate or professional students. All FWS positions are paid on an hourly rate.

Since this is a need-based program, the financial aid office will tell you whether you qualify for a position and the amount of money you are eligible to earn through the work-study program. If you do qualify, then you have to go out and find a position that is work-study eligible. Departments usually are happy to hire work-study students, because the department has to pay only a small portion of the salary, and the rest is paid by the federal government.

Loans

Unless you have your own resources or you receive full funding from the school, you will need to borrow to finance your education. Typically, about 75 percent of students pursuing a professional degree will borrow some money to attend school. Contrast this to graduate school where free money is more available, and you will find just about 50 percent of graduate students borrowing to finance some portion of their expenses. As costs have risen and loan caps have increased, there has been an explosion of student borrowing in the last few years. This has led to great concern about whether students are borrowing more than is prudent.

If you live like a professional while you are a student, you will live like a student when you are a professional. Lavish spending now can mean debt and credit problems later on when you are trying to establish yourself as a professional and may be wanting to buy a house and start a family.

Borrowing the least amount of money possible is wise and requires that you plan and budget carefully. One obvious way to borrow less money is to save as much money as possible before attending graduate or professional school. Professional students usually find that loans are their primary source of financial aid, while graduate students often can get a significant portion of their costs covered by grants. Loans come from two basic sources: the federal government and private lenders. Details of each of the loan programs can be obtained from the lenders (Chapter 11 provides contact information). This chapter will provide a brief overview of salient features of the different loan programs. These loans are:

- Federal Perkins loans
- Federal subsidized Stafford loans
- Federal unsubsidized Stafford loans
- William D. Ford direct loans
- Private loans
- Institutional loans

A disclaimer is important at this point. All information about loans is correct at the time of writing, but loan programs can change, depending on the government and on the private lenders, so you will need to check with your school and lenders to get the most up-to-date information on loan terms.

To qualify for a federal loan, you have to be a U.S. citizen or permanent resident, be registered for the draft (if you are a male), not be in default on any prior federal student loans, and complete the Free Application for Federal Student Aid (FAFSA).

Federal Perkins Loans

If you can get a Federal Perkins loan, you should take the money and run. Perkins loans are the most desirable loans because they have an extremely low interest rate (currently 5 percent), and the interest is subsidized (paid for by the federal government) while you are in school and during your grace period. This loan is need-based, and your eligibility will be determined by the financial aid office.

Perkins loan funds are rather limited, and some universities choose not to award Perkins money to graduate and professional students but to restrict the use of that money to undergraduate students. The maximum amount that can be borrowed from the Perkins program is only $5,000 per year, so you should not assume that the Perkins money will be able to pay for all of your costs. The cumulative maximum you can borrow in Perkins loans is $30,000, including undergraduate school.

After graduation, you will have a grace period of six or nine months (depending on when you received your first Federal Perkins loan) before you have to begin repaying the loan. The interest is subsidized during the grace period, so it is a nice way to ease yourself into the working world and begin saving some money before you have to start making payments.

You can ask the schools that interest you whether they offer Perkins loans to students in your program, and if so, how much they typically give to students each year.

Federal Subsidized Stafford Loans

Subsidized Stafford loans are the most common loans for graduate and professional students. Although the interest rate is not as low as for the Perkins loan, it is lower than for other loans, and the interest is subsidized while you are in school and during the grace period. Like the Perkins loans, these loans are need-based, and your eligibility will be determined by the financial aid office. Unlike the Perkins loan, the amount of money available is not limited, so all eligible students can borrow the full amount of their eligibility. Graduate and professional students can borrow a maximum of $8,500 per year through the Subsidized Stafford Loan program.

Although the federal government sets a standard government interest rate, some lenders may choose to charge lower rates for these loans. The interest rate varies annually and as of July 1, 1998, is based on the 10-year Treasury Note plus 1.0 percent, per annum. The good news is that the interest rate is capped at 8.25 percent.

Federal Unsubsidized Stafford Loans

Federal unsubsidized Stafford loans are also guaranteed by the federal government, but the government does not subsidize the interest while you are in school. You have the choice of making interest payments while you are in school, or, a more common choice, letting the interest accrue while you are in school and then be added to the principal balance upon graduation. These loans are not need-based, so you can borrow them even if it is determined that you are not needy.

Unsubsidized Stafford loans are generally more desirable than private loans, because the interest rate is lower. During repayment, the interest rate is the same as the interest rate for the subsidized Stafford loan. From the time you borrow your loan until you go into repayment, the interest rate is based on the 10-year Treasury Note, plus 1.0 percent, per annum, capped at 8.25 percent.

The maximum amount that you can borrow from the unsubsidized Stafford loan program is $18,500 per year, minus any amount that you borrowed as a subsidized Stafford loan. As an example, if you are eligible to borrow the full $8,500 as a subsidized Stafford loan, you would only be able to borrow $10,000 ($18,500–$8,500) as an unsubsidized Stafford loan. The cumulative maximum you can borrow through the subsidized and unsubsidized Stafford loan programs combined is $138,500.

If you are attending medical school, the maximum yearly amount you can borrow from the unsubsidized Stafford loan program is $48,500, minus any amount that you borrowed as a subsidized Stafford loan. This is a new loan limit that is a response to the government's discontinuance of the Health Education Access Loan (HEAL).

When you borrow a Stafford loan (either subsidized or unsubsidized), you will be charged two fees: an origination fee and a guarantee fee. Both fees will be deducted from the amount of money you are borrowing, so if you are borrowing $18,500, you won't receive that exact amount. The origination fee is 3 percent of the amount borrowed and is paid to the federal government. The guarantee fee is paid to the guarantor of the loan and varies depending on the lender; however, it cannot exceed 1 percent.

You have a six-month grace period after graduation to begin repaying your Stafford loans, and you have ten years to pay off the loans. Through consolidation, the repayment period may be extended to up to 30 years.

William D. Ford Direct Loans

William D. Ford direct loans are virtually the same as the Stafford loans, except that the federal government is the lender. The interest rates, borrowing limits, and availability of subsidized and unsubsidized money are just the same as for the Stafford loans. Each school participates in either the federal Stafford loan program or the direct loan program, so you will not have a choice between the programs; your school will have made the choice for you.

Private Loans

There are a number of private lenders who have established loan programs specifically for graduate and professional students and their parents. These loans help to fill the gap between the maximum amount of money that is available from other sources and the university's cost of attendance. Rates and terms vary on these loans, although they are not as desirable as the federal loan programs.

Many of the lenders have programs specific to each of the disciplines; for example, they will have separate loan programs for medical students, law students, graduate students, and business students. Some of the more common lenders are The Access Group, Citibank, Nellie Mae, and The Education Resources Institute. Information about these lenders is available from the schools to which you are applying. Contact information is also provided in Chapter 11 of this book.

Although lenders may offer slightly different terms on Stafford loans, the terms will not vary greatly due to the government regulations surrounding those loans. The terms offered by private lenders can vary greatly, however. When selecting a private lender, you should find out as much information as possible about the terms of the loan and about the lender. Questions to ask include the following:

- What is the interest rate on this loan? Is it fixed? If not, when will it change (quarterly, yearly, etc.)? If it is variable, is there a cap on the amount of interest you can be charged?
- What are the guarantee or insurance fees for this loan? Lender A may charge a 9 percent fee when the loan is disbursed (so that amount is deducted from your loan proceeds), while Lender B will only charge 6.5 percent at disbursement but will charge an additional 2.5 percent when you go into repayment.
- Will any of the fees be reduced or eliminated if you obtain a co-signer on the loan?
- When do you have to start repaying the loan?
- If you have credit problems, you should ask what the approval criteria are for the loan, so you know whether you need to look for another lender that will loan you money despite your credit history. You may not be able to find such a lender.
- How reliable is the lender? Has the lender been in business a long time? Is the lender accessible to applicants and students through toll-free telephone numbers, e-mail, the Internet, or other means?
- Does the lender offer repayment incentives that will reward you if you make your payments on time for a certain period of time or if you have your loan payments automatically deducted from a checking or savings account?

- How long will you have to repay the loans? Typical repayment terms are 15–20 years, and some lenders allow you to make your payments for up to 30 years.

The following table might help you compare the different loan programs and give you a better idea of the differences and similarities between them.

Type of Loan	Subsidized	Interest Rate	Grace Period	Need-Based?	Credit Check
Perkins	Yes	5.0%	6 or 9 months	Yes	No
Subsidized Stafford	Yes	Capped at 8.25%	6 months	Yes	No
Unsubsidized Stafford	No	Capped at 8.25%	6 months	No	No
Private Loans	No	Variable	9 months	No	Yes

Institutional Loans

Some schools offer their own loan programs for students. These can either be full-blown programs that are designed to take the place of private loans, or they can be much smaller programs that are designed to be used only if you can't get your needs met through other loan programs or for specific circumstances. Since the existence, terms, and conditions of these loans vary widely, the only way to find out about them is to ask each school.

Applying for Aid

If you plan to apply for federal aid (Perkins or Stafford loans or Federal Work Study), you must complete the Free Application for Federal Student Aid (FAFSA). As the name implies, the FAFSA is free and will be sent by the FAFSA processor to the schools you designate. The FAFSA cannot be completed until after January 1 of the year you are applying for aid. You can complete either a paper version of the FAFSA or you can apply electronically using the Web site: **http://www.fafsa.ed.gov**.

You will need to have completed your tax return when you fill out the FAFSA. It's common for people to put off filling out their tax returns (most people can think of more fun ways to spend their time), especially if they aren't expecting a tax refund, but if you're applying for financial aid, you should complete the return as soon as possible after January 1.

Be sure to enter the correct school codes on the FAFSA, so the right schools will receive your information. You want the code for the program you are entering, which may be different from the university's code. If you have any doubts, call the financial aid office to find out the correct code for that school.

Once you have completed your FAFSA, you will receive a Student Aid Report (SAR). The SAR indicates what information you included on the FAFSA and reports an estimated family contribution (EFC), an amount the school uses to determine your Stafford loan eligibility. You should read it carefully to make sure that all of the information is correct. If you have submitted incomplete or conflicting information, the SAR will tell you what to do to correct it.

After you receive your SAR, it is a good idea to check with the schools to which you are applying to make sure that they also received a copy of the SAR. Many schools are set up to receive SARs electronically, but the system doesn't always work as well as it should, so it pays for you to double-check and make sure it has been received. The school can't do anything to process your federal aid unless it has your SAR!

In addition to the FAFSA, check with individual schools to see if they have their own applications that must be completed or if they require you to complete an additional form provided by a third party. These supplemental applications are typically used by schools to award their own institutional funds. As noted earlier, they may ask for information about your parents' income and assets. Just because you consider yourself to be independent of your parents doesn't mean the school will do the same.

All schools also require you to submit a financial aid transcript (FAT). Schools that admit you will send you a copy of the FAT. You will be required to complete the top portion of the form and to send it to the financial aid office at all of the schools you have attended in the United States since graduating from high school, regardless of whether you applied for or received aid from that school. Your college will send the FAT to your graduate school. Be kind to your undergraduate financial aid office and give plenty of time to complete the FAT. A few weeks after you have submitted your FAT to your undergraduate school, you should call your graduate school to find out if it has been received.

When you are admitted, some schools will tell you immediately how much free money they are offering you, while other schools will wait for a few weeks or a few months. If the school has its own scholarship application, you will have to complete that before the school can let you know the amount of your award. You generally will not hear about the federal loans you are being offered until sometime after March. This is due to the fact that the school has to wait until it receives your SAR before it can tell you how much federal money you can get. Sometimes schools can estimate the amount of federal money you will receive, so you can call and ask if you haven't heard anything in a reasonable amount of time.

The school will send you an official award notice at some point in the spring (hopefully before you have to make a commitment to the school about whether you will attend there). You will need to indicate on that sheet which financial aid you accept and which you don't want to accept. You usually have to sign the form and return it to the financial aid office. Be sure to read the form and follow the directions.

You might wonder why you would accept only some forms of financial aid and not others. The reason is that you have to decide what makes the most sense for you financially. Even though a school might offer you enough loans to cover the entire cost of attendance, you might have $3,000 saved and your parents might give you an extra $2,000. If the school did not take that $5,000 into account when it offered you a loan package, you can subtract that $5,000 from the least attractive loan and only accept the other loans that have been offered.

Josie received a financial aid award from a school that said her total cost of attendance would be $25,000 for one year. Her EFC was $1,000, so they offered her $24,000 in financial aid. It was broken down as follows: $2,000 scholarship; $8,500 subsidized Stafford loan; $10,000 unsubsidized Stafford loan; and $4,500 private loan. When she looked at the school's total cost of attendance of $25,000, she thought that she could save $4,000 by living in a cheaper apartment than was allowed and spending less on entertainment. She decided not to accept the private loan.

If you accept any type of loans as part of your financial aid package, you still have to get loan applications and complete those. Usually you send the applications to your school's financial aid office, which certifies that you are a student and that you are eligible for the loans for which you are applying. The school will then send the applications to the lenders.

Remember to request loan applications from your school or from the lenders. You should generally complete the applications in May or June.

Determining Financial Need

To determine your financial need, schools will look at your income from the previous year and your assets. They will use those figures to determine how much money you should be able to contribute to your education for the following year. They will subtract that amount from the cost of attendance they have determined for their school. The resulting figure is your financial need that can be met through some type of free money or through loans. Unless you are able to document special circumstances to the financial aid office, you will not be able to borrow more than that amount.

You may be surprised at the school's cost of attendance, because it may not seem like enough money for you to live on for a year. However, it behooves you to live within that budget and to spend even less money than called for, if possible, to minimize the amount of loans you need to take. Many students borrow money rather blithely, not thinking about the repayment ramifications until they are suddenly faced with a large amount of debt.

Mary felt like she had to have a car for medical school. Since she didn't already own one, she went out and bought a relatively inexpensive car, but the monthly payments were still $200. Robert, on the other hand, also didn't have a car, but he made the decision that he could live close enough to school to walk and that he would supplement that by taking the bus and taxis when necessary. Although it would have been far more convenient to have a car, he realized that it wasn't a necessity and he decided not to spend that extra $200 per month that Mary was spending (plus the cost of insurance, parking, gasoline, and upkeep).

Are Admissions Decisions Need-Blind?

Sometimes people are concerned that if they apply for financial aid, that fact will be taken into account when they are considered for admission and their admissions chances will be lessened. All but a very small handful of graduate and professional schools practice need-blind admissions. This means that an applicant will be admitted regardless of his or her financial situation.

If you do apply to a non–need-blind admissions school, you may find that you will not be admitted because your debt load is too high. Alternatively, you may be admitted, but once the school finds out that you will be unable to finance your education through loans, your offer of admission may be rescinded.

At a need-blind admissions school, your need for financial aid will be considered only after you have been admitted. Sometimes this can mean that you will be admitted to a school you cannot afford, either because your undergraduate loan debt is so high that you won't be able to borrow the money needed to complete your graduate education, or because you have poor credit and will not be able to borrow any credit-based loans. If this should happen to you, it will mean that even though you have been admitted to the school, you will not be able to attend there, because you cannot afford it.

Joe was told before he started business school that he would be unable to borrow the entire cost of his education because he had poor credit. He insisted that he would be able to get the money from other sources. Then during the second semester of his first year, he went to the financial aid office complaining that he didn't have enough money and asking the school what assistance they could offer him. The office told him that he had made the decision to attend that school, knowing that he couldn't afford it, and if he couldn't find any other money, he would have to withdraw.

Credit-Worthiness

Most of the private lenders check your credit history and will not allow you to borrow money if you have a history of poor credit. Thus, it is important to make sure that your credit record is clean and that you have no problems. You can do that by requesting a copy of your credit report from the various credit reporting agencies. Information on them is listed in Chapter 11.

If you find that you have credit problems, ask the financial aid office if they have advice for resolving them. Since financial aid officers have dealt with numerous students over the years; they often know how you can make a change on your credit report if there is an error or how you can work with a lender to overlook your credit report.

> Since you have to reapply for loans each year, you must keep your credit record clean throughout your time in graduate or professional school to ensure that you will be able to continue receiving loans throughout the duration of your schooling.

Credit card companies love to tempt people, particularly students, with seductive offers of credit that are sent unsolicited through the mail. When you receive these offers, tear them up and throw them away. Don't be tempted to open numerous credit card accounts. One account should be sufficient for your needs, and the credit limit should be kept to no more than $1,000. Use this credit card judiciously, and pay off the balance in full every month. Do not carry a balance on your account that will accrue interest, or you might be paying off that balance for a very long time.

Typically, lenders will look at the following factors when determining your credit-worthiness:

- the number of accounts that have been 30, 60, 90, or more days delinquent in the last two to five years
- whether you have a charged-off account (an account that the lender has had to write off because it was deemed to be uncollectible) or a collection
- whether you have had a foreclosure, repossession, loan default, or bankruptcy in the past seven years

Repayment

When borrowing money, be sure to look at the repayment plans and the anticipated amount of your monthly payments. Consider your future income to determine whether it is realistic for you to be able to make those monthly payments. The following chart gives you an idea of your monthly payments, based on a 9 percent interest rate and different repayment periods.

Total Amount Borrowed	10-year repayment	15-year repayment	20-year repayment
$10,000	$126.68	$101.43	$89.97
15,000	190.01	152.14	134.96
20,000	253.35	202.85	179.95
25,000	316.69	253.57	224.93
30,000	380.03	304.28	269.92
40,000	506.70	405.71	359.89
50,000	633.38	507.13	449.86
60,000	760.05	608.56	539.84
70,000	886.73	709.99	629.81
80,000	1,013.41	811.41	719.78
90,000	1,140.08	912.84	809.75
100,000	1,266.76	1,014.27	899.73

If you anticipate that your initial income will be low but will increase steadily, you may want to ask the lender about the availability of a graduated or income-sensitive repayment schedule, which would allow you to make lower payments in the early years when your income is low and higher payments as your income increases.

If you find at any time during the repayment period that you are having difficulties making your payment, contact the lender to find out what options are available to you. If you simply stop making your loan payments, your loan will go into default, and this will be reported to all national credit bureaus. This type of negative information in your credit report will make it difficult, if not impossible, for you to get loans for other purposes, like a car or a house.

The lenders want to work with you to help you repay your loans. Even if you make only a fraction of your payment each month, it's still better than not making any payment. There are three main ways that you can get help with paying back your loans. One is to consolidate your loans; the others are to get a forbearance or a deferment from your lender.

Consolidation

A consolidation loan does just what it sounds like. It consolidates all of your federal loans (Stafford, direct, and Perkins) into one loan. When you consolidate your loans, you get a longer period of time to make your payments, which reduces the amount of each monthly payment. It also increases the overall amount you will pay, because of the extended repayment period. When you consolidate your loan, you will have a new interest rate, which may end up being higher than the variable rate you would have been charged in some years on your individual loans. You may extend your repayment period up to 30 years.

Forbearance

You can ask your lender for a forbearance if you are experiencing temporary financial difficulties. If the forbearance is granted, the lender will reduce your loan payments for a fixed period of time. The interest will continue to accrue during this period, so you will ultimately end up owing more money, but this is better than going into default.

Deferment

If you get a deferment, your loan payments will be temporarily suspended. Deferments are granted for three reasons: you are enrolled at least half-time in an institution of higher learning, you are unemployed, or you are experiencing economic hardship.

Loan Forgiveness

Some schools offer loan forgiveness or loan repayment assistance programs. These programs are designed to assist graduates who want to take lower-paying jobs in the public sector. These programs are relatively common in law schools, although the details of the programs vary greatly from school to school. The basic principle of all of the programs is that if you take a certain kind of job (in law school, that usually means working for the government or a public interest agency) and your salary is below a certain level, the school will give you money to help you pay back your loans. The money the school gives you may be an outright grant or it may be a loan that has to be paid back only if you don't continue working in the public sector for a certain defined period of time.

Conclusion

As you have surmised from this chapter, financial aid processes and procedures vary greatly from school to school. Therefore, you need to ask, ask, ask each of the schools about their policies and procedures to make sure that you understand how they handle financial aid. Don't assume that all schools are the same or that the answer you get from one school is the same as the answer you will get from another.

Important Facts for Dealing with Financial Aid

- Complete the FAFSA as soon as possible after January 1.
- Check with each school's financial aid office to determine whether the school has a specific financial aid application that must be completed.
- Meet all deadlines established by the schools.
- Complete paperwork promptly.
- Communicate regularly with the financial aid office to make sure that you have received all of the forms and have filled them out correctly.
- Keep your debt as low as possible.
- Be diligent and creative in seeking out alternative sources of funding.
- Keep only one credit card that has a low credit limit. Limit its use to emergencies, not everyday items like going out to eat or buying groceries.
- Have a savings account that is separate from your checking account and that is difficult to access. This will make it harder for you to spend money from that account that you haven't budgeted to spend.

Financial aid is clearly an important factor to consider when you are deciding which school to attend. This chapter should have given you all of the tools you need to assess that criterion. The following chapter on "Choosing a School" will discuss other factors to investigate when you are trying to make the final decision of where you want to receive your degree.

Financial Aid Worksheet

As you are deciding among various schools, you can use the following worksheets to help you compare how much it will cost you to attend various schools and what type of aid you are being offered. You can use one set of worksheets for each school you are considering and then compare the results.

Estimated Income	
Savings	$________
Trust Funds	$________
Family Members (parents, spouse, grandparents)	$________
Scholarships/Grants/Fellowships	$________
Estimated Tax Refund	$________
Work-Study	$________
Assistantship	$________
Other Work (including summer earnings)	$________
Federal Perkins Loan	$________
Federal Subsidized Stafford/Ford Loan	$________
Federal Unsubsidized Stafford/Ford Loan	$________
Other Loans	$________
Other Sources	$________
Total	$________

Estimated Expenses	
Tuition (annual)	$________
Fees (annual)	$________
Books/Supplies (annual)	$________
Housing (monthly x 12)	$________
Food (monthly x 12)	$________
Utilities (monthly x 12)	$________
Telephone (monthly x 12)	$________
Insurance (annual)	$________
Transportation (monthly x 12)	$________
Entertainment (monthly x 12)	$________
Medical/Dental (annual)	$________
Clothing (annual)	$________
Laundry/Dry Cleaning (monthly x 12)	$________
Child Care (monthly x 12)	$________
Credit Card Payments (monthly x 12)	$________
Other	$________
Total	$________

chapter 9

Choosing a School

Congratulations! Now that you have applied and been admitted to a number of schools, you have the biggest decision of all to make. You get to decide which school to attend. Since you will be spending anywhere from one to seven years at this school and you will be associated with it as an alumnus for the rest of your life, you clearly need to spend a great deal of time thinking about where you will be happiest.

This is an exciting time for most people, because they feel as if they are finally in complete control of the process. While you may get a lot of advice from friends and family, you are the one who makes the final decision about where you will spend the next chapter of your life. Chapter 4 talked about factors to consider when applying to a school and used the analogy of a pyramid. Now that you have been admitted, you are about to reach the peak of the pyramid where your choice will be narrowed down to one school.

At this point, there are additional factors for you to consider. You should also reconsider the factors you took into account when you were deciding where to apply. The fact that a school's campus is not very pretty might not have been important to you when you applied, but now that you have been admitted to a number of schools that are relatively equal in other ways, you may decide that the beauty of the campus will be a significant factor in your decision of where to enroll.

If you have not yet visited the schools to which you have been admitted, now is the time to go. Look at everything while you are there, and talk to as many people as possible, including students, faculty, and staff. Look with a discerning eye, and try to imagine yourself at that school. If you feel some uneasiness as you try to envision yourself going to school there, try to figure out what's causing those feelings and whether it's really the right school for you. You will be spending a number of years attending the institution you choose, and you should not do it without first seeing the schools.

Dan consciously and methodically visited ten schools during the summer after his junior year. He wanted to see them before he applied to determine whether he wanted to apply there. He liked nine of them but couldn't see himself attending the tenth, yet he still applied to that school. When I asked him why he applied to a school he didn't like, he said that it was such a good school, he felt like he had to apply. That seemed like a waste of his time and money and of the school's time. The point of your visit should be to determine if you would like the school. If your visit shows that you wouldn't like it, there's no reason to apply.

Visit a school before deciding to enroll there.

There are a number of stories about students who chose a school without visiting it first and when they arrived for the first day of school, they immediately realized that they had made a mistake. You can make sure that this doesn't happen to you by visiting the school before you decide to attend there. Each school has a different feel, and it is impossible to know what that feel is without visiting a school. When choosing a school, you should think carefully about yourself and your likes and dislikes to determine whether a particular school will meet your needs and whether it will allow you to thrive and meet your full potential.

When you first started thinking about attending graduate or professional school, you probably sought out advice from friends, family members, trusted professors, and others. People probably offered unsolicited suggestions, as well. Now that you have been admitted to a number of schools, you might be overwhelmed with advice. Keep in mind that while much of this counsel can

One year I received a call very late in August from a student who had been admitted to the school where I worked. She said that she had been admitted to my school but had turned down our offer. She instead chose to attend another school that was closer to home and a bit less expensive. However, she had never visited that school, and when she moved there to start classes, she knew that she would not enjoy the campus's very urban atmosphere. She asked if it was too late to change her mind and enroll at my school instead (which she also hadn't visited!).

be useful, no one else has the same point of view that you have or wants the same things that you want. You have to filter all of that advice through your own set of values and needs. It doesn't matter whether your mother attended a school and thought it was wonderful or whether your best friend is at a particular school and is having the time of his life. What matters is whether *you* will be happy there.

The following questions are ones you might ask yourself when you visit a school. Not all of them will be important to you, and of those that are important, they may not be of equal importance. Only you can decide what matters the most to you. The main issues to keep in mind are:

- Interaction
- Stress level
- Library
- Campus facilities
- Location
- Cost
- Size
- Strengths or specialties
- Reputation
- Student body
- Faculty
- Interaction between program and rest of campus

- Employment options
- Mission
- Learning environment
- Safety

Interaction

The amount and type of interaction that you see among students and faculty can tell you a great deal about the character of a school. Although you may be more independent or more retiring than others, you should look for a decent level of interaction at the school, both within the student body and between students and faculty. Remember, no matter how brilliant you are, you will be learning from the other students and from the faculty outside of the classroom, so you need to know how accessible those people are to you. Look around as you visit the school, and ask yourself the following types of questions:

- Do you see students interacting with each other in the hallways?
- Do you see students and faculty interacting with each other in the hallways?
- Do faculty members have their doors open or closed?
- Are office hours posted, which may mean that faculty are only available during those hours, or are there no hours posted, which may mean either that faculty are never available or that they are always available?
- Are there plenty of common areas?
- Are the common areas designed to encourage interaction?

Stress Level

Some level of stress is to be expected during graduate and professional school. You would be abnormal if you experienced no stress. However, some schools are more stressful than others, either because they foster competition or because they are so intellectually challenging that they allow no time for other social pursuits. You may thrive in a competitive environment, or you may prefer one that is more nurturing, or at least more cooperative. The following questions can help you to get some idea of the stress level students seem to be feeling at the schools you visit.

- Do the students seem happy?
- Are the students friendly and warm and open?
- Do the students complain incessantly about the school but say it's worth it because it's so highly ranked?
- Do you sense a spirit of camaraderie and cooperation among the students or is there more of a sense of distance or mistrust?
- Do students seem to know each other and to talk freely, or is conversation muted or nonexistent?

Kerry decided to visit schools during finals time, because she thought that would be the best time to gauge the stress level of the students. She hoped to find a school where, even during finals, students were relatively happy and not neurotic. She noticed a real difference in the atmospheres at various schools and was able to find the one that best suited her. Knowing what is important to you will allow you to make similar judgments about the right school for you.

Library

Depending on your field of study, the library may well be your home for the next several years. Now that so many resources are available online, you will probably want to know as much about the school's ability to access those online resources as you will want to know about its book collection. You will also want to think about whether you will be using the library primarily for research (in which case the collections will be most important to you) or whether you will be using it primarily as a place to study (in which case the physical facility will be most important to you). Some questions to ask as you look at the library are:

- Are the computer facilities adequate for the number of students?
- Do students study in the library or do they use it as a place to socialize? If you want to study there, but it's not quiet, that may be a problem for you.
- Does your specific discipline have its own library?

- What is the quality of the holdings? Although most schools tout the quantity of their holdings, the quality is more important, since a school's holdings may consist of many obsolete or obscure books that will not be useful to you.
- What is the quality of the library's periodical holdings? This is often one of the first places where a library makes cuts in a budget crunch. Periodicals won't necessarily show up in a library's holdings description. An updated periodical selection can be very important, especially in rapidly changing fields such as biochemistry or oncology. By the time the "latest" findings are reported in books, they are often obsolete.
- How many reference librarians are there, and how accessible are they to you?
- Does the library have carrels? Is the number adequate for the number of students who want to use them? Are they big enough for the type of work you want to do in them?
- How comfortable is the library seating?
- Does the library have the type of study facilities you like best: either reading rooms with long tables or lots of nooks and crannies where you can hide yourself away and feel like you are alone?
- How is the lighting in the library?
- As a graduate or professional student, can you be assigned your own carrel or locker within the library so you don't have to carry all of your books back and forth?

Campus Facilities

You may or may not be interested in the facilities offered by the campus outside of your department. If your school is self-contained within its own building and offers most of the services that you would normally get from the central administration, you may not care about the rest of campus. However, if you want to or have to interact with the university outside of your own department, you may want to pay attention to the rest of the campus to see if it meets your needs. In some cases, usually with professional schools, your school may be physically separated from the rest of campus, sometimes by miles. If this is the case, you will have a very different experience than if your school is part of the university campus. If the school is separated, it is highly unlikely that you will take advantage of cultural, social, or athletic events offered by the university, even though you may technically be eligible to use them. Some questions to ask include the following:

- Are the campus facilities that interest you (gym, student union, sporting venues) located near where you will be taking classes?
- Can you take advantage of all of the campus facilities?
- How far is your school from the rest of the university? Are you on the edge of campus, right in the middle of campus, or separated from the campus by a number of miles?
- What is the process for getting tickets to athletic events? At Duke University, undergraduates have to camp out for some games in order to get a ticket, while graduate and professional students only have to camp out once at the beginning of the season in order to get season tickets.

Location

The location of the school is another factor to consider, beginning with whether it is in an urban or a nonurban location. Location can affect the type of job opportunities and social activities that are available to you while you are in school. Location also influences the cost of living while you are attending school. If you want to spend your free time (what there is of it) outdoors, don't choose a school in a big city. If your idea of unwinding is going to major cultural events, a school in a more rural location probably won't suit you. Questions to ask include:

- Are the activities I enjoy likely to be found here?
- What kind of housing is available—dormitories, upscale apartments with swimming pools and tennis courts, typical college town apartments, rental houses?
- How heterogeneous is the community?

- What type of social, cultural, and recreational activities are offered by the school and the community?
- How is the weather? If you're a Floridian who hates the cold, you may not be able to stand Chicago winters.

Cost

Cost of living plus cost of tuition, fees, and other expenses is certainly an important factor to consider. In fact, for many people, cost may be one of the most important factors. When looking at costs, be sure to take into account the types and amount of financial aid that you are offered and subtract that from the total cost of attendance at each institution. Do not just compare the tuition costs at the different schools. Financial aid is covered in great depth in Chapter 8, so if you need a refresher, reread that chapter now. Financial aid is most important at this stage of the process when you are actually choosing which school you will attend. Questions to think about are:

- What is the average cost of housing in the area? What is the low end (and what are you getting for that cheap rent) and what is the high end?
- What will your travel costs be if you want to visit family during holiday breaks?
- Do you need to have a car to get around in a particular community? If you already have one, you can just include the cost of upkeep. If you need to buy a car, you need to decide whether you can get by with a cheap clunker until you have finished school or whether you want to buy a more expensive car that will eat into your budget more.
- If you're going to go to school in a city and plan to take a lot of cabs, how much will they cost?
- How much is entertainment? Movie prices range from $6.00 to $10.00 in different areas. The cost differential can add up quickly.
- How much do groceries cost?
- If you plan to eat out a lot, think about the cost of restaurants in the area.

During Susan's first year of medical school, she lived in the graduate and professional student dormitory and took advantage of the school's meal plan. Unfortunately, the meal plan did not operate on the weekends, and the school was located in the heart of an expensive part of the city. Since she couldn't afford to eat in the expensive restaurants nearby, didn't have time to travel to cheaper restaurants in other parts of the city, and couldn't have cooking equipment in her dorm room, she ended up eating lots of canned tuna fish on the weekends. By the end of the year, she vowed never to eat tuna fish again.

Size

The size of the school matters to some students. Larger schools may offer more course offerings and a wider selection but may also be more impersonal. Smaller schools may provide the opportunity to get individual attention from professors but students may feel stifled if they think that everyone knows everyone else in the class.

When considering size, think about both the size of the program you will be in and the size of the classes you will take. While three schools could have an entering class of 200 students, one school might divide the students into two sections of 100 students each, the next school might divide the students into five sections of 40 students each, and a third school could divide them into three sections of 65 students each. For most students, the number of students in a course is as important or more important than the number of students in the entering class.

Ask about the number of students enrolled in individual courses. Don't just ask about the size of the entering class.

Typically, in graduate and professional school, the size of the university does not matter as much as the size of the program you will be entering. However, even with two similarly sized programs, some students may prefer to be situated within a larger or a smaller university. Although you may not have to deal with the university bureaucracy much as a graduate or professional student, it is important to find out how much you will have to deal with it and how "friendly" it is to graduate and professional students. Most universities are set up to handle the needs of undergraduate students first, since they comprise the vast majority of the students there. Thus, if you find that your program provides little internal support for areas like financial aid, registrar, career services, and others, you should be especially careful to find out how the central university treats graduate and professional students and to find a place where you can be happy.

Once he enrolled at University A, Gary found that while his financial aid was handled by the law school during his first year (because it was related to recruitment), it was handled by the university's financial aid office during his last two years. Since the university's financial aid office was not located in the same building as the law school and the financial aid people were not particularly helpful, he found handling financial aid during the last two years to be much more trying than during the first year.

Obvious questions related to size are:

- How many students are enrolled at the university?
- What is the proportion of graduate and professional students versus undergraduate students? If the proportion is low, you might find that your needs as a graduate or professional student are not considered very seriously by the university.
- How many students are enrolled in your program?
- What is the average number of students enrolled in individual courses? Does the number change from required courses (usually taken in the first year) to upper level courses?

Strengths or Specialties

Depending on the type of degree you are seeking, you may want to pay attention to whether the school you are considering has particular strengths or specialties. Are they good in areas that interest you, or is their specialty in an area that doesn't appeal to you at all? Since this topic was probably one that you considered when you were first deciding where to apply, it was covered at some length in Chapter 5. You might revisit the subject at this point, especially if during the application process, your thoughts have changed about what you want to do with your degree.

Reputation

Reputation was discussed extensively in Chapter 4; however, it pays to look at the issue again now. Specific rankings should play a negligible role in your decision making at this point. You certainly don't want to make the mistake of choosing a school that is ranked number nine over a school that is ranked number ten, based solely on that ranking. The most important thing is that the school have a good reputation and be well regarded in the area where you want to work. One way to find out more information about the school's general reputation is to talk to alumni of the school or to talk to people practicing in the field and get their input. For example, if you are considering a PhD program, talk to other PhDs about the programs you are considering and the general reputation of the schools. You might specifically ask:

- Is this school known for a particular area, such as 18th-century literature or intellectual property law?
- How strong is the school's reputation in the location where you think you want to work?
- Are graduates of this program highly regarded?

Student Body

You will be spending a lot of time learning from and socializing with your classmates. Make sure that you are compatible with them and that they represent a wide spectrum of the population. The best way to discover this is through talking to students when you visit the campus. You may also care about how students dress. This would be particularly true, for example, if you favor a very casual, perhaps grungy look, and all of the students dress in a very preppy manner. You could ask the following types of questions to ascertain what the students are like.

- Are they from geographically diverse places?
- How many of them came right from college, and how many took time off?
- What kinds of work experiences have they had?
- Do most of the students seem to have the same ideological bent, i.e., mostly conservative or mostly liberal?

Faculty

Faculty are clearly a key ingredient in the experience you will have while in graduate or professional school. When thinking about faculty, the number one consideration is how good they are, both in their profession and as instructors. You want to attend a school where you will learn from people who are at the top of their profession and who are genuinely interested in your intellectual progress and maturation.

Ideally, faculty members would be genuinely interested in their teaching, accessible to students in their offices, and spend time doing "important" work outside of the academy, whether that is lecturing, consulting, or conducting research on timely topics. Of course, it can be difficult for a professor to do all three things. She can't be lecturing in Afghanistan, for example, and still be there to talk to you after class at the same time. However, schools can do things that make it easier for professors to achieve both results by requiring them to be in their offices a certain amount of time or mandating office hours. Simply creating a culture where faculty are expected to be accessible to students can make a difference.

It will be relatively easy for you to find out about professors' publishing records and their scholarly activities from materials published by the school. The only way to find out about their accessibility and their skill in the classroom is to ask current or recently graduated students. The written materials might say that they have superb teachers who are always in their offices willing to talk to students, but the students can tell you whether that is actually true.

You should be careful if you choose a school based primarily on the fact that a particular professor teaches there and you are interested in working with or taking a class from that professor. You may be surprised at how often professors don't teach at their universities, either because they are on sabbatical, research leave, or are "visiting" at another school. If you are seriously interested in a specific professor and you would feel very disappointed if you were unable to take one of that professor's classes, you may want to find out his or her proposed leave schedule. Also keep in mind that students often change their minds about the field of study they want to pursue, so unless you are absolutely certain that you want to study a particular area, it is probably not wise to choose a school based primarily on the presence of one or two specific faculty members.

Other questions to ask include:

- Are faculty members currently involved in interesting research?
- How recent are their publications?
- Did they publish prolifically a number of years ago but have been resting on their laurels for the last several years?
- Are faculty members more interested in teaching or in research?
- What is the faculty-to-student ratio?
- How diverse is the faculty in terms of age, gender, race, scholarly interest, background, and political persuasion?
- Are there ideological "camps" among the faculty?
- Do faculty members listed in the course catalog actually teach, or are they merely "window dressing" for the school? A prominent Midwestern university has a well-known writer listed in the catalog, and students who go there to take a course from him end up disappointed, because he doesn't actually teach any courses there.

Interaction Between Your Program and Rest of Campus

You may want to know whether your program is involved in a significant way with the rest of campus, either through faculty involvement or being included with joint ventures with other departments. Activities with other departments and schools within the university can broaden the number of intellectual and social opportunities that are available to you.

Dan was enrolled in the law school, but he wanted to take a couple of classes at the business school to strengthen his finance background. He found out that the law school would accept the credits he earned at the business school toward his law degree. Since the business school was right next door to the law school, it was easy for him to fit the business classes into his regular law school course load.

As was discussed in the "Campus Facilities" section, where your school or department is physically located on the campus can make a real difference to the amount of interaction you can have with other schools or departments at the university.

Questions you can ask to help you determine the level of interaction between your school and the rest of the university include the following:

- How many joint degree programs are offered? The more joint degree programs there are, the higher the level of interaction will be between your school and other parts of the university.
- How many faculty members have joint appointments? This means that they have an appointment at your school and an appointment at another school in the university.
- Does your school's catalog show courses that are cross-listed with other departments? This means that students from your school and the school where the course is cross-listed can both register for the course without having to take any special steps.
- Does your school ever sponsor any social events with another school?

Employment Options

You most likely wouldn't be attending graduate or professional school if you weren't looking to enter a particular field or get a particular kind of job. Therefore, you should look carefully at the employment experiences of those who have gone before you at potential schools. The admissions office should be able to give you employment information about recent graduates. If they don't have the information, they should be able to tell you where you can get it. Chapter 10 will tell you what types of jobs you can get with various degrees and will give you an overview of the job market.

Most professional schools will have their own career services offices. If they do not, that may be a signal to you that the school does not take employment opportunities for its graduates very seriously. If a school does not have its own career services office, you should be able to use the services of the university's career services office. Find out if they have anyone within the office designated specifically to work with students in your program. Ask what services they offer.

Most graduate schools will not have their own career services offices, and students will rely mostly on professors for advice and assistance when they are seeking jobs. Thus, it may be much harder to get centralized information from a graduate school about where recent graduates are working. You may have to rely more on individual faculty members' recollections than on actual written records. Don't be surprised if faculty members know more about the fate of recent PhDs than recent MAs. Professors are generally more vested in the careers of their PhD students because those programs last so much longer than MA programs.

Although most people have some idea of why they want to attend graduate or professional school, they often don't know exactly what they want to do with their degree after they graduate. Career counseling can help tremendously in this area. Ask the schools what career counseling services they offer and how available they are to students.

Donna went to medical school thinking that she wanted to be a neurologist. Once she enrolled in school and got more exposure to that area, she decided that that wasn't the specialty she wanted to study. She was worried that she didn't know enough about other areas of medicine to make an informed decision about what specialty to pursue, and she didn't want to make another mistake. When she went to her school to get some advice, she found that there was no career services office where she could get sufficient information about different medical specialties. They also had no one trained to help her figure out her own interests and values and how they might mesh with a medical specialty. She ended up talking to a number of doctors who practiced in different areas and trying to get advice from them. Since their primary mission was not to help her determine her path in medicine and each had a rather limited view of the type of work he or she was doing, she found the experience to be frustrating and time-consuming.

Ask where recent graduates are working, both in terms of the type of employment they have (if most students from a particular school go to work for the government immediately after graduation and you want to work for a company, that school may not be right for you) and the location. If you only want to work in California, it may not be wise to attend a school where most of the graduates go to work in the northeast. Some other questions are:

- What are the starting salaries of recent graduates at the schools you are considering?
- How many graduates were employed at graduation in the previous year? How many were employed three, six, nine, or 12 months after graduation?
- How involved are faculty in helping students find satisfying jobs? In graduate school, many of the job leads come through faculty members, so it is important to know how willing they are to be helpful and to advocate on your behalf.

Mission

Some schools have a professed mission and some have an implied mission. If a school's mission is to train doctors to practice in rural areas and you want to practice in a large, urban hospital, that school is not right for you. Ask whether the school has a mission, and then determine if that mission meshes with your values.

When inquiring about this area, the first question to ask is simply whether the school has a written mission statement. The admissions office can provide this information to you. If the school does not have a written mission statement, you can try to find out if there is an unwritten mission statement by asking the following questions:

- Do most graduates of the school work in one particular area? If so, you might assume that the school is doing something obvious or subtle to encourage graduates to choose that career path.
- Does the school have a religious affiliation? If so, does that affect the philosophy of the school in any way?

Learning Environment

What kind of learning environment does the school foster? You will find that just as you are engaging in a process of searching and introspection to choose the school that is right for you, students before you have done the same thing. Thus, there is a process of self-selection at schools that tends to lead to the same type of students choosing the same school. If you learn best in an atmosphere where the students are collegial and supportive, don't choose a school where there is a strong sense of competition.

Related to the learning environment is the *attrition rate* (the number of students who start in a program but don't graduate). If there is a high attrition rate in your program, ask why. The school may have a philosophy that it should admit a large number of students and then weed them out once they have started. Alternatively, the school may be too rigorous for many of its students. It also may be a place where students are unhappy so they choose to attend another school where they will be more comfortable. Whatever the reason, it's important for you to know what it is and decide whether it might affect you.

Questions to ask in this area might include the following:

- How many students who start in the program continue on to graduate from it?
- What are the reasons that students do not continue in the program?
- Does the school encourage or even mandate a lot of group interaction (most MBA programs have a significant component of group work)?
- Is there an attitude that students should be able to study and learn on their own and faculty members are just there for occasional guidance and direction, or is there a sense that faculty are truly engaged in the learning process of their students?

Safety

Safety can be a major factor for some students. You will be unlikely to find an administrator who will tell you that a campus is unsafe. They might couch their answer by saying, "Well, every place has some safety issues," or "Of course, being located in a large city, we have some of the same safety issues as other big cities." Your best source of information regarding subjective safety concerns is current students, as they can tell you about their experience at the school. The campus police department can give you statistics about crimes that have happened on campus within the last year or so. You can also just look around the campus to determine how safe it seems to you.

Questions to think about with respect to safety include the following:

- How safe is the campus?
- Are the access routes to the library, from the parking lot, bus stop, or dorms, well lit? Patrolled?
- Is there an escort service for students?
- Are emergency telephones located across the campus?
- If you plan to study late at night and will be driving to campus, is there parking located near where you will be studying?
- What are the building's security systems, for example, are buildings locked all the time, and only those with access cards can enter, or are they locked at 5:00 p.m., or not until 11:00 p.m.?

Now that you have considered all of the factors listed above and determined how they apply to you, there are some additional issues that you may want to consider if you are specifically thinking about law school, medical school, business school, or graduate school. Those issues are discussed in the following paragraphs.

Law Schools

Special factors to consider when looking at law schools include the following:

Does the school offer clinical programs? If you are interested in getting practical, hands-on experience or want to represent low-income clients while you are in law school, a clinic is the best way to do that. There are typically two types of clinics where you will have "live clients." One is sponsored by the law school, and students are supervised by faculty members. The clinic may be located at the law school or somewhere off campus, but the important fact is that you will be directly supervised by faculty members. The other type of clinical experience a school might offer is where you work for an agency that has been approved by the law school. In that case, you will be directly supervised by an attorney working at that agency. The school will have some kind of arrangement where a faculty member will periodically check on your work but typically won't have any kind of direct supervision over you.

In lieu of offering a clinic, some schools might offer pro bono programs, where the school has agreements with agencies in the area for students to do legal work for that agency on a volunteer basis. Some schools have mandatory pro bono programs and others have voluntary programs. The breadth and depth of these programs can vary widely from school to school, so if you are particularly interested in this type of experience, ask a lot of questions.

What moot court programs does the school offer? In moot court, students are paired up and presented with a "made-up" case that has already been decided at the trial level and is on appeal to a higher court. You and your teammate are assigned to represent one of the parties in the lawsuit, and you have to write a brief and then argue in front of a panel of judges. Moot court is a way to get experience with appellate brief writing and oral advocacy and can be a great training ground. Most schools offer at least one major moot court competition in which students can participate; some offer a number of programs in specialized areas.

Every school has a law review, a very prestigious activity in which to participate. A law review is a journal that publishes scholarly articles written by faculty members and students. Law reviews are almost always totally student-run, so students get to decide which articles to publish, edit those articles, and produce the journal for publication. Students are able to participate on the law review based on various criteria—writing competition, grades, or a combination of both. Many schools also offer specialized law reviews in different areas of the law that can give you the opportunity to write about a topic in which you have a particular interest.

Does the school offer academic support programs in case you need additional help during your time there? Academic support ranges from informal programs where the dean of students or another administrator will find help for you if you need it to very structured programs that last for the first semester or the first year. Sometimes these programs are open only to students whom the school thinks might need extra help, based on their undergraduate GPA or test score.

Medical Schools

An important factor when considering medical schools is the quality of the hospital associated with the medical school. Since much of your training will actually happen in the hospital, you want your medical school to be associated with a hospital that has good equipment and facilities. Also look at the number of hospital beds available for teaching purposes and the type of hospital that is used (private, city, or state).

Most medical school professors are practicing physicians, so you should find out where their primary interests lie. Are they interested more in teaching, in research, or in doing clinical work? If their primary interest is research or clinical work, they may not spend much time on their teaching and may not be very interesting lecturers.

The nature of your relationship with faculty members in medical school will be somewhat different than in other programs. Many of your courses will be taught by multiple instructors, who will come in and lecture about discreet topics; the faculty-student relationship is not as important during the first two years of course work as it is in most other programs.

Business Schools

One way to get practical experience while you are attending business school is to work on a consulting project for a local company as part of a course. The beauty of this approach is that if you are doing the project as part of a course, you are getting credit for it, but since the professor has already arranged for the project, you don't have to go out and find it on your own. Depending on the location of the school and the number of nearby companies , these projects will be more or less common. If you are interested in getting this type of experience, ask the school how common it is there.

Some business schools use advanced math in many of their courses. If you are math-phobic, you may want to find a school that uses only basic math or that insures that all students' math skills are up to the heavy mathematical analysis required.

Teamwork was mentioned briefly in the general factors under "Learning Environment," but it deserves further attention here, since many business schools make extensive use of teamwork. If you would rather work alone than work with others, you should ask about the teamwork requirements at the school. Find out if you must work in a team in almost every class or if teamwork is only used in some classes, perhaps electives that you could avoid if you chose to do so.

Graduate School

When selecting a graduate school, the most important consideration is the faculty. Although the topic of faculty was covered in the general considerations section of this chapter, it deserves special mention in the graduate school section. In graduate school, you will have an adviser who will be your main contact in graduate school throughout the two to seven years you are enrolled there. Although you don't necessarily have to know the exact person you want to be your adviser before you enroll, you should know that there are a number of good people from whom to choose. Don't assume that a world-renowned professor is going to be good for you to work with. This professor may be brilliant, but he or she may also be arrogant and not interested in mentoring and nurturing graduate students. You will be closely associated with your adviser throughout your professional career. People will know who you studied with and will link you with that person, even if you don't have much contact with him or her anymore.

In addition to an individual adviser, you will also need other professors to serve on your thesis or dissertation committee. Typically, for a master's degree, you will need two professors to review your work; for a doctoral degree, you will need at least five people. Ideally, they would all be interested in the same things you are interested in, but that isn't always possible. You should at least make sure that there are enough faculty members with interests related to yours that they will be willing to serve on your committee and be helpful to you.

How congenial are faculty members with one another? Since more than one faculty member will be sitting on your review committee, you need to know that they are capable of getting along and won't decide to make your thesis or dissertation part of a bigger battle going on between them. If the department has deep political divisions, you could get caught in the crossfire without doing anything to cause it.

One last issue to consider regarding the faculty and the department you are exploring is the stability of the department. If the department has a lot of young, rising stars, they might be wooed away to teach at other schools during the time that you are enrolled in the program. If the core of the faculty is near retirement age, the faculty will be very different when you graduate than it was when you started.

As with professional schools, there can be opportunities to get practical experience before you graduate. If you are in a program that requires or suggests clinical or field work, find out what types of opportunities are offered at each school. If you are in a program with a heavy research component, find out what kinds of grants the school gets to support the kind of research you would like to do. If you plan to teach after receiving your degree, ask how easy it is to get a teaching assistantship in your field (this topic is covered in greater depth in Chapter 8 on financial aid).

If you are enrolled in a program that requires supervised fieldwork, make sure that your adviser will be actively involved in supervising you and will give you good advice throughout your fieldwork placement. You don't want a professor who says that everything is "fine" while you are going through the placement, only to find out at the end that there were problems that could have been resolved sometime during the placement.

Conclusion

If you absolutely cannot visit a school, and again, I stress the importance of finding the time and money to go, try to find out as much as you can about the school in other ways. Contact the admissions office and ask for names of current students who attended your undergraduate school or are from your hometown. You can also ask for names and phone numbers of alumni working in an area that interests you. If you find that a school is unable or unwilling to put you in touch with current students or alumni, that can tell you a lot about the school and how much it values its relationship with students, alumni, and you, a prospective student.

You can also contact faculty members who are working in your field to ask about their research and to get some idea of how much compatibility there may be between you and them. Most professors have e-mail addresses and/or voice mail, so they should be easy to reach. You may have to be persistent, though, as they may not return your e-mail message or telephone call immediately. Again, the way you are treated by a faculty member can tell you something about the school, or at least about that particular professor.

The Chamber of Commerce can be a good source of information about the area and possibly has publications with pictures. Pictures can tell you a great deal about the nature of a location and can help you envision it even if you can't visit.

If you thoroughly investigate the schools to which you have been admitted, as outlined in this chapter, you should find the decision-making process to be exciting and empowering. Where you go to school is your choice. By going through the process of clarifying your needs and deciding which school can best meet them, you will prepare yourself to approach graduate or professional school with confidence and enthusiasm. As you are going through this process, it may be helpful for you to use the following worksheet. It includes all of the decision criteria discussed in this chapter. You can decide which of the criteria are most important to you and then can rank the schools on those criteria that you want to consider. Then you can see which school rates higher on the factors that are most important to *you*. Good luck with your decision!

Decision Criteria	School A	School B	School C	School D
Interaction				
Stress Level				
Library				
Campus Facilities				
Location				
Cost				
Size				
Strengths or Specialties				
Reputation				
Student Body				
Faculty				
Interaction Between Program and Rest of Campus				
Employment Options				
Mission				
Learning Environment				
Other Factors				

Section 4

Moving On

chapter 10

Job Options

This book wouldn't be complete without talking about what you can do with your graduate or professional degree after you have earned it. Since most people attend graduate or professional school because they want to do something different with their lives, it's important to have a realistic idea of what kinds of opportunities might be available to you after you graduate. It is very disheartening to see someone who has spent a great deal of time and money getting a degree only to find out that there are very few jobs available in that field or that the graduate isn't interested in that field after all.

Many people choose graduate or professional school as a sort of default position. They aren't sure what else to do with themselves, and they think that having an extra degree will make it easier for them to get a job. They often haven't thought much about what type of work they actually want to do and whether it is necessary to get an additional degree to be hired in that field. By carefully exploring the kinds of job options that might be available to you if you earn a particular degree, you can save yourself from that situation.

Think about potential jobs *before* you enter graduate or professional school.

When reading this chapter, it's important to keep in mind that job availability can be cyclical, so an area that has plentiful jobs now might not have many jobs by the time you graduate and vice versa. It's also true that the type of job you can get is dependent upon many factors, including where you go to school, who you study with, the types of research and work experiences you have while in school, and the grades you earn. Thus, although this chapter won't allow you to create an exact blueprint of your career path, it will give you a general idea of the kinds of opportunities that are available.

It is wise to remember that there are thousands of people in this country using their graduate and professional degrees in ways they never could have imagined while they were in school. To a great degree, people create their own paths in life, and this is true with your career as much as with anything else. Thus, you may well have a medical degree and decide that you don't want to be a physician but want to work in the health policy arena. Although you probably don't want to be a taxi driver who has a PhD, you also don't want to define your career options too narrowly. Since there are hundreds of "nontraditional" ways that people can use their graduate and professional degrees, this chapter will focus primarily on the traditional ways of using those degrees.

Many professions—law, medicine, and social work, to name a few—have licensing requirements, so you have to be tested after you earn your degree in order to receive a license to work. Licensing requirements vary from occupation to occupation and from state to state. You may want to have a general idea of licensing requirements before you begin your program.

Law School

Lawyers are involved in almost every aspect of our society. They are necessary if you have to go to court, write a will, draft a contract, or start a business. Lawyers provide advice and counsel in a large number of situations. The lawyers you may have seen on *Law and Order, L.A. Law,* or *Perry Mason* are not typical of the practice of law in that they represent only a small portion of the legal profession. The American Bar Association (ABA) reports the following statistics on the employment of lawyers in different types of organizations:

Attorneys By Field	
Private practice	72.9%
Business/corporations	9.5%
Government	8.2%
Legal aid/public defenders	1.1%
Legal education	1.0%
Retired/inactive	4.6%

The pattern of employment is somewhat different for recent graduates, although the largest percentage of graduates still enter private practice. The National Association for Law Placement (NALP) reports that somewhere between 49 percent and 65 percent of lawyers took their first job in a law firm over the last 20 years. For the graduating classes of 1993–1994 and 1994–1995, the three most common types of positions after private practice were judicial clerkships, the government, and businesses, with approximately 12 percent of the graduates choosing each of these three.

The ten states that have provided the largest number of jobs to new graduates have remained the same from 1990–1996. New York has had the largest number of jobs during that period, and California has had the second largest number of jobs. The position of the other eight states has fluctuated somewhat within the top ten, but the other eight states are Illinois, Texas, District Columbia, Florida, Pennsylvania, Ohio, Massachusetts, and New Jersey.

The median starting salary for the class of 1996 was $40,000, with the medians ranging from $30,000 for public interest jobs to $50,000 for jobs in private law firms. Although people often see large dollar signs when they think about being a lawyer, only 11 percent of new lawyers make more than $70,000.

Types of institutions where lawyers might work are private law firms, business and industry, government (including the judiciary), academic institutions, and public interest organizations. We'll discuss each of these categories so you can get a general idea of what you might be doing if you were working as an attorney for one of these organizations.

Private Law Firms

The largest number of lawyers in this country work in some form of private practice, which means that they work for law firms. These firms may be solo practices or they may be large firms employing hundreds of attorneys. Smaller law firms may specialize in one area or they may handle all kinds of cases. Large firms are usually divided into departments and attorneys are assigned to a department where they specialize in a particular area.

Business and Industry

Businesses and corporations encounter many types of legal problems. Small companies usually hire lawyers from law firms to work with them on an as-needed basis. Large companies will have their own lawyers who work for the corporation and give advice and guidance as legal matters arise. These lawyers are called *in-house counsel.* Businesses need lawyers if they buy or are bought by another company, they want to sell stock in their company, they want to form a corporation, they buy property, or they want to sue or are sued.

Government

Government lawyers can be found working for local, state, and federal agencies. Government agencies face many of the same legal issues that businesses face. They enter into contracts, hire employees, purchase land, and are sued by people, all of which may require the services of an attorney. Every federal government agency has lawyers working for it. Lawyers can also be found in great numbers in policy positions in the government and many lawyers hold elected office.

Peter practiced law for many years with a private law firm and with a government agency, and then he was appointed by the governor to serve as the secretary of the department of natural resources for a large western state .

Judiciary

The judiciary deserves special mention because judges are so prominent in our society and because a popular job choice for recent law school graduates is a judicial clerkship. Judges may be elected or appointed, and they may serve for a set period of time (five or ten years) or they may have a lifetime appointment. They can be found deciding cases at all levels, from local traffic courts to the United States Supreme Court. All federal and many state judges hire judicial clerks to help them with their duties. Judicial clerkships are one- to two-year positions for recent law school graduates. Clerks will research the issues presented by the parties who are suing and they will write memos to the judge outlining those issues. They may also write the first draft of a judge's opinion.

Academic Institutions

Lawyers who work in academia may be teaching at the law school or they may be teaching law or another subject at the undergraduate level. They may also be working as an administrator in higher education. It is very common now to find lawyers working in law schools as deans and directors of admissions, career services, student affairs, and development. Lawyers also hold these types of administrative positions within the university as a whole. Of course, universities also have their own attorneys, who act in a similar position to in-house counsel for a corporation.

> Amanda practiced law for a few years and then was hired by a law school to serve as its director of career services. As a lawyer, she had been very involved with hiring new associates for her firm, and she also was interested in the counseling side of her law practice. Working for the law school gave her a way to combine her interests in hiring and counseling.

Public Interest

Public interest agencies include organizations like the ACLU, Business and Professional People for the Public Interest, and Legal Aid. Attorneys working for public interest agencies are usually working on behalf of clients who cannot afford representation. They may represent individuals in situations like landlord-tenant disputes or Medicaid eligibility, or they may work on more of a systemwide basis setting policy or designing systems that will better serve the needs of the poor and disenfranchised.

Legal Specialties

Lawyers who work in any of the above types of positions may be generalists who have to know something about many areas of the law, or they may be specialists who focus on only one area. Some legal specialties that we will discuss are international law, environmental law, corporate law, employment law, intellectual property law, trusts and estates, and litigation. There are numerous other legal specialties that you may choose to pursue, including tax law, family law, construction law, entertainment law, criminal law, constitutional law, and civil rights law.

When Connor graduated from law school, he went to work for a law firm. He thought that he would work in the tax area, because he had enjoyed tax classes in law school. Once he got there, he was assigned to work on a case involving a construction company, and after five years, he discovered that his expertise was in construction law, an area about which he had known nothing when he graduated from law school.

International Law

International law encompasses both private and public issues. Private international law is concerned with relationships between individuals or companies that want to do business overseas. International lawyers may work with U.S. corporations that have offices outside of the United States, or they may have clients who are international corporations that want to do business in the United States. If you work in public international law, you may work on human rights issues or on laws like GATT (General Agreement on Trade and Tariffs).

Environmental Law

If you work in environmental law, you may work on behalf of individuals or organizations who want to preserve the environment in a particular state, or you may work to defend a corporation against charges of pollution or advise it on how to comply with environmental regulations. The environmental area is full of regulations, so people who want to work in this area should be especially good at reading and analyzing laws.

Many people are attracted to the area of environmental law because they want to "save the Earth" or have similar strong feelings toward protecting our natural resources. However, most of the jobs available in environmental law are working for corporations that may be trying to find ways to get around environmental regulations.

Corporate Law

Corporate law is a very broad category that includes almost all aspects of a corporate business. This includes drafting and interpreting contracts, dealing with tax law issues, helping an organization with finance issues such as bankruptcy or reorganization, advising a client on securities law issues, or helping a client to merge with or acquire another company.

Employment Law

If you work in employment law, you may be representing individuals who have been discriminated against on the job or who otherwise have a complaint against their employer, or you may be representing an employer against such charges. You may also advise an employer on applicable employment laws and how to hire, promote, and fire people legally. Labor law is a component of employment law which involves the laws governing labor unions, including collective bargaining.

Intellectual Property Law

Intellectual property law is a hot area now with the expansion of the Internet and all of the related legal issues. Intellectual property law is concerned with the rights of people to their own work, as represented by copyrights, trademarks, and patents. Copyright attorneys work with authors, artists, and others to counsel them on their rights to the works they have created. They can negotiate contracts for their clients and can go to court to enforce their copyrights. Patent lawyers generally must have an engineering or science background, because they need to understand the technical aspects of their clients' inventions in order to help them get patents.

Trusts and Estates

If you work in the area of trusts and estates, you will help people write their wills and plan for their estates. There are many tax vehicles that are advantageous to people in dealing with their estates, and you will help them decide which vehicle is best for them.

Litigation

Attorneys who are litigators represent clients who are suing or have been sued. Most people's common image of a lawyer is of someone standing in a courtroom. The reality is that a small percentage of lawyers ever see a courtroom, even if they are litigators. Criminal lawyers (both defense and prosecution) are in court all the time, whereas corporate litigators tend to settle many cases before they reach trial, so they seldom go to court.

There are many other specialties and places of employment for lawyers, but the above sampling should give you a good taste of the possibilities available to you if you decide to pursue a law degree. Next, we'll turn our attention to medicine to see what job options you might have if you earn a medical degree.

Medical School

During your senior year of medical school, you will apply for a residency. As part of this process, you will interview with the hospitals that interest you. At the end of the interview process, you will create a prioritized list of your top choices for residencies. The hospitals will create their own prioritized lists of the candidates they have seen. These lists will then be "matched" by the National Resident Matching Program, and you will be assigned to a residency based on that match.

The first year of your residency is called an internship and usually will be general in nature. Near the end of your internship, you will take Part 3 of the United States Medical Licensing Exam. It will ask questions related to the clinical management of patients in the hospital. You will begin to specialize after your first year.

Residency Choices of Medical School Graduates	
Internal medicine	27%
Family practice	12%
Pediatrics	11%
Surgery	10%
Obstetrics/gynecology	8%
Psychiatry	6%
Orthopedic surgery	5%
Radiology	4%
Emergency medicine	3%
Anesthesiology	3%
Others	11%

You can expect to earn between $20,000 and $45,000 per year as a resident, depending upon your hospital and location. During your first year of residency, you will usually have to work between 60 and 100 hours per week and will be on call every second, third, or fourth night. After the first year, your on-call schedule can vary greatly, depending on your specialty. Dermatologists and anesthesiologists are rarely on call, while pediatricians and surgeons are on call frequently.

As indicated in the following table, residencies can be quite long. They also can be quite demanding. You have probably heard horror stories of how hard residents must work and of the long hours they must put in. Some hospitals have made their residencies a bit more humane, and New York has instituted a law that says residents may not work more than 80 hours a week, but working 80 hours a week still doesn't leave much time to sleep, eat, or take care of the details of life.

Number of Years Required to Complete Residencies	
Internal medicine	3
Pediatrics	3–4
Surgery	5–8
Obstetrics/gynecology	4–5
Psychiatry	5

After you complete your residency, if you want to subspecialize in a particular field, you will have to do a fellowship that can last an additional three to eight years. As you can see, practicing medicine is not for the faint of heart or those who don't want to commit a number of years to the endeavor. Fellowships are desirable to some people because doctors with subspecialties usually make more money and are considered to have more prestigious jobs. It's also easier for doctors who have specialized to keep abreast of everything that's current in their field.

After you spend three to eight years in a residency, you will need to spend another three to eight years in a fellowship if you want to have a subspecialty.

Just as the legal shows on television are not representative of the practice of law, shows such as *E.R.* and *Chicago Hope* are not representative of the practice of medicine. The largest number of doctors today are engaged in solo practice. They may be truly solo, where they are the only doctor in the office and they are completely responsible for all aspects of the business, or they may have an associateship where they share an office with another solo practitioner. Another model is a solo practitioner associated with a health maintenance organization (HMO).

There are drawbacks and benefits to being a solo practitioner. A disadvantage is that you are responsible for building your practice (unless you buy an existing practice), and you don't necessarily have a ready stream of patients coming in the door as soon as you open for business. You also have to hire your own staff and complete a lot of paperwork for insurance claims. The biggest advantage to having your own practice is that you have the autonomy to run your practice exactly as you want to run it without interference from anyone.

The next most popular practice arrangement after solo practice is group practice. In this model, three or more doctors use the same staff and office, and they divide the income of the practice in a mutually agreeable way. Doctors in a group practice tend to work shorter and more regular hours than solo practitioners, because they can make arrangements with their colleagues to take some of the load and they can rotate the on-call schedule among them.

The next largest group of doctors work for an organization that pays them a salary. These organizations may be HMOs, hospitals, insurance companies or other businesses, or the government. Although this type of practice is not prevalent among all doctors, it is a popular choice for doctors who are beginning their practices. Over half of doctors begin working as a salaried practitioner and then they start a solo practice or join a group practice. Approximately six to eight years after they begin practice, fewer than one-third of doctors remain in a salaried position.

When Susannah graduated from medical school, she joined a managed health care organization because it seemed like a good way to get mentoring from other doctors and to have a guaranteed client base. After five years, she found a practice that was being sold by a retiring doctor, and she purchased it.

This employment pattern may be changing, however, as the role of managed care becomes more prevalent in our society. According to the American Medical Association, 36 percent of doctors worked for HMOs in 1990. By 1995, that figure had climbed to 64 percent. The role of managed care has become a troublesome issue for many doctors and has made the profession less attractive to some. Almost all doctors, even those who have a solo practice, are affected by managed care. This is because they may have a relationship with a managed care company and get some of their patients via that route. Managed care companies place a number of restrictions on doctors, including what tests they can perform, how much time they can spend with patients, what labs they can use, and even what medications they can prescribe.

Some doctors will choose to work as *locum tenens* (Latin for "place holder"). As a *locum tenens* doctor, you work as a substitute. You may either be substituting for a doctor who is on vacation for a few days or you may be working for a few months in an area that has not been able to find a full-time doctor. Some new doctors like these temporary positions, because it gives them the flexibility to travel around the country and to get a number of different experiences. Older doctors can also choose this type of employment, especially if they are seeking a change in their lives or are nearing retirement.

Another employment avenue for doctors is teaching and research. Research is a crucial activity for those with medical degrees as they seek to find causes of and cures for diseases. Researchers' work is often funded by grants, so they spend a fair amount of time seeking those grants.

Jonah worked for a hospital doing research into hearts: how they work, how they get diseased, and what can be done to prevent heart attacks and other heart problems. Although he worked for a hospital, his research was funded by grants, and he was responsible for obtaining those grants. If the grants ended, so did his employment.

Unlike lawyers who never have to declare a specialty or study in a particular area in order to specialize in it, doctors select their specialty when they select their residency and then their fellowship if they choose to pursue one. While it is possible to change specialties, it is not easy, especially if you are far into your training. Thus, it is important for medical students to explore carefully the many specialties that are available and choose wisely. This chapter will cover a few of the more common specialties, including internal medicine, family practice, pediatrics, surgery, obstetrics/gynecology, psychiatry, radiology, and emergency medicine.

Although about half of all residents enter a primary care specialty (family practice, internal medicine, and pediatrics), the American Medical Association says that there aren't enough doctors working in general and family practice and that there are too many anesthesiologists, dermatologists, pediatricians, psychiatrists, radiologists, surgeons, and urologists. Another result of managed care is that the need for primary care physicians has grown, since managed care systems use primary care physicians as gatekeepers to the rest of the medical system. It used to be that a woman could go to an OB/GYN when she was pregnant and then continue going to her for other medical problems after the pregnancy. Now managed care systems won't allow that and will require the woman to see a primary care physician first who can then refer her to an OB/GYN if she has a problem requiring the services of that type of doctor.

Internal Medicine

Doctors who specialize in internal medicine are concerned with the medical problems experienced by adults. You have to be able to diagnose and treat many different kinds of adult illnesses and need to know when to refer a patient to a specialist.

Family Practice

If you become a family practitioner, you will have a broad specialization rather than a deep one, because you will have to know all about every disease that everyone in a family might get. Your patients will range from infants to the elderly, and you will be asked to diagnose and treat many types of disease. You will also have to decide when it is appropriate to refer your patient to a specialist who will be better able to treat the patient's illness.

Pediatrics

Pediatricians deal with the illnesses of children. Having a personality that will put your patients at ease is particularly important for pediatricians, since children can have a difficult time dealing with illness and doctors. Pediatricians may also deal with behavioral problems like child abuse, drug addiction, and suicide prevention. Since many of the cases seen in emergency rooms are children, pediatric emergency care is a growing specialty.

Surgery

Surgeons operate on people who need to have a part of their body repaired. You may choose to specialize in a certain type of surgery, such as heart surgery, orthopedic surgery, or transplants, or you may perform general surgery. Laser surgery has become quite popular and common for many types of operations that used to be performed in a more invasive way.

Obstetrics/Gynecology

Obstetricians and gynecologists (OB/GYNS) deal with medical issues that are unique to women including pregnancy and childbirth. Because so many unexplained medical problems can happen to fetuses and newborns, and because people are much more willing to sue, some small towns have trouble finding OB/GYNS.

Psychiatry

Psychiatrists are MDs who have chosen to specialize in diseases of the mind and brain. As a psychiatrist, you may work directly with patients providing therapy or you may do research into mental illness.

Radiology

Radiologists are responsible for using x-rays and similar tools like CAT (computerized axial tomography) scans and PET (positron-emission tomography) scans to diagnose illnesses. Some of the new tools that are available in this area are magnetic resonance imaging (MRI) and ultrasound.

Emergency Medicine

If you have seen the doctors on *E.R.,* you may think you know all about emergency medicine. Doctors who work in emergency medicine have to be able to withstand a great deal of stress and make quick decisions. It is not a place for someone who needs to ponder at great length before rendering a decision. As an emergency room physician, you will be exposed to a number of different kinds of medical problems, so you will have to know something about many areas.

Although there are many other medical specialties you could choose, the sampling provided here includes the more commonly selected specialties. Now we'll look at what kind of employment you might find if you decide to get an MBA degree.

Business School

As with most programs, the demand for MBAs is cyclical. Sometimes MBAs are in high demand and everyone wants to hire them. At other times, they are considered less desirable. There was concern at one point that an MBA wouldn't enhance one's employment prospects. However, given the large number of MBA programs and graduates (who have a vested interest in promoting the value of MBAs), it is likely that the demand will remain relatively high.

Starting salaries for MBAs can range from $36,000 for someone who has a nontechnical undergraduate degree and no prior experience, to $54,000 for someone who has a technical undergraduate degree and a few years of experience.

Companies that hire MBAs on a regular basis have a clear idea of why they are hiring them and what they can do for their companies. They may have a formal training program for their MBA hires. They often prefer to hire people who have prior experience in their industry. If they are hiring people with previous experience, they are not hiring them for their technical expertise in the area but for their ability to provide leadership and management. Companies that don't hire MBAs on a regular basis may need the person with the MBA to take more initiative in determining what kinds of tasks can be accomplished and what value the MBA can add to the organization. These companies usually don't have a formal training program and expect their hires to learn on the job.

Industries that traditionally have hired the largest number of MBAs have been consumer goods, management consulting, and financial services. MBAs can also find jobs with the government, educational institutions, and smaller companies, including high-tech start-ups. Some MBA graduates start their own companies.

MBA graduates are usually given responsibility for strategic planning, setting policy, personnel issues, and financial decisions, including investments. MBAs could have more of a general focus that encompasses a number of different areas, or they may find themselves working in one area and becoming increasingly specialized in that area. Some of these areas are human resources, finance, accounting, marketing, information systems, and operations management. We'll cover each in turn.

Human Resources

Every organization has a need for someone to perform human resources functions, which encompass the hiring, promotion, and retention of staff. Human resources offices have expanded beyond those duties, however, which is why they are now called human resources and not personnel. The human resources function now includes areas like affirmative action and equal opportunity, total quality management, and staff development. Developing and administering employment policies is clearly an important component of a human resources office.

Finance

If you want to work in the finance area, you may be hired by a large corporation or a financial institution, where you could be involved in all issues of money management. If you are a corporate financial manager, you will look at how the corporation is using its financial resources and make recommendations for how they can be used more effectively. You may also look at the cash flow of the company and make decisions about wise investments. If you work for a financial institution (typically a savings and loan or a bank), you may work as a trust officer and advise people on their investments or you may work as a loan officer where you decide whether the institution will loan money to an individual or organization.

You may also work for an investment bank where you could help organizations restructure their finances through mergers, acquisitions, or other devices. You will also give advice to companies about how to invest their money.

Accounting

You may decide to earn your MBA because you are already a Certified Public Accountant (CPA) and you want to broaden your perspective, or you may earn the CPA designation after you get your MBA and begin working in accounting. As an accountant, you will be responsible for keeping track of the financial activities of an organization, including its revenues and expenses. As an MBA you will usually be involved in the policy aspects of accounting, which can include analyzing the financial aspects of the company, making recommendations for the procedures to be more accurate, or forecasting future expenses.

Marketing

A major source of marketing positions for MBAs is in the area of brand or product management. As a brand or product manager, you will be responsible for all aspects of one product produced by a company, including the manufacturing of the product as well as everything related to the marketing of the product. In the beginning, you will usually work as a member of a small team of managers who are assigned to a product. If you choose to focus on marketing, you may also be employed as a sales representative, a market analyst, or a media planner. Another area of employment is advertising agencies, where you can plan and develop advertising campaigns for clients.

Immediately after graduation from an MBA program, Melissa was hired to work in the marketing department of a small subsidiary of a large corporation that produced labels and tags. She started out working on all aspects of marketing for this company, including going to trade shows to market the company's products. She eventually worked her way up to be head of the marketing department, overseeing four employees and thinking strategically about how to position the company to get the greatest market share in a competitive environment.

Information Systems

The use of information technology has exploded within our society, and there is a great need for people who can manage the use of that technology. If you choose to work in the information systems field, you can expect to act as a conduit between the information systems department and other departments in the company by translating the technical information into terms that nontechnical people can understand. You will also make policy decisions about what hardware and software systems to purchase, how information should be stored, and who should be able to access it.

Operations Management

Manufacturing operations hire MBAs to serve as operations managers. As an operations manager you will be responsible for all activities necessary to produce a company's products. This means you will have to develop and manage efficient systems for dealing with the company's machines, employees, and suppliers.

The functions of MBAs that were described above can be performed in many different types of settings. Some of the areas lend themselves to particular types of organizations, as outlined in those descriptions, but others are applicable to a variety of organizations. Since many people think of MBAs working only for corporations, it is worth mentioning some of the other types of organizations that can hire MBAs. They are educational institutions, government agencies, health care organizations, nonprofit agencies, and management consulting firms. You could also start your own business.

Educational Institutions

Just as law schools will hire lawyers to serve in administrative areas like admissions, career services, and development, business schools will hire MBAs to serve in those roles. You may also be sought for financial positions with universities or with public school systems.

Patti got her MBA degree and was hired by the College of Arts and Sciences to serve as the administrative dean. She was responsible for managing the budget for the entire college, acting as the conduit to the university personnel office, and handling all issues related to the physical plant.

Government Agencies

You may be hired by a local, state, or national government agency to help the agency run more efficiently in terms of its use of materials, personnel, and money. You could also be hired as a human resources specialist or for your marketing expertise.

Health Care Organizations

Hospitals and HMOs clearly need MBAs to assist them with the business problems of running their organizations. With rising competition and increased health care costs, these organizations need MBAs to help them run more efficiently and market their services effectively. Some MBA programs even offer a concentration in health that would make you more appealing to a hospital or HMO looking to hire an MBA.

Nonprofit Organizations

All kinds of nonprofit agencies can benefit from hiring MBAs, since they are faced with similar problems as for-profit organizations. You could help a museum generate more revenue by writing a marketing plan that would attract more people to the museum, or you could help a symphony write a financial plan.

Management Consulting Firms

You may be hired by a management consulting firm to provide advice to clients on a whole range of business issues. Management consulting firms may specialize in the types of problems they address or they may be generalists.

Entrepreneurship

No discussion of MBA employment opportunities would be complete without discussing the role of entrepreneurs. Self-employment has grown tremendously in this country, and having an MBA can help people be more successful when they launch their businesses and can help them be more aware of the problems inherent in running a business. Many entrepreneurs will work in a salaried position when they first graduate and then will start their own business, while others will jump right into business upon graduation.

As part of Ron's MBA program, he had to write a marketing plan for a business. He had been repairing chipped crystal for a number of years, and he decided to write the marketing plan for that activity. When he had finished it, he realized that he had a viable business opportunity staring him in the face, so when he graduated from business school, he made his crystal repair sideline into a full-time business.

Graduate School

People have a number of reasons for earning a master's degree. You may be so interested in a subject that you want the opportunity to study that subject in depth. You may not necessarily be looking for a job in that field but are just expanding your intellectual horizons. You may also get a master's degree because it will help you advance in your field. You may already be working in an area (social work, computer science, or engineering, to name a few) and know that if you have a master's degree, you will be able to advance more quickly. You may also want a master's degree because you want to get the credentials to break into a new field of work. You also might choose to get a master's degree if you want to teach in secondary school. Obviously your reason for pursuing a master's degree will, to a large extent, dictate the type of job you will seek after graduation.

The situation is different for PhD students, since traditionally, people who pursued a PhD, especially in the arts and humanities, planned to teach. Numerous articles have been written in the last few years about the bleak nature of the academic job market for PhD candidates. Of course, once you get your PhD in eight to ten years, the market could be quite different, so you need to think about how much your decision making should be affected by what is happening in the job market now. As a prospective PhD student, you should clearly do a lot of research into the nature of jobs received by recent graduates at the schools you are considering and should be realistic with yourself about what kind of job you would be happy taking. If you think you would only be satisfied in a tenure-track position at a four-year institution, you should be very choosy about the school you attend and ask careful questions about its placement track record, to make sure that you aren't disappointed a number of years down the road.

If you are getting a PhD so you can teach in a tenure-track position, be very aware of the poor job market for those kinds of positions.

Much of what you will be able to find out about the PhD job market will be anecdotal because there is no one organization that collects data on employment of PhDs. Some of the statistics that are available on this subject should also be subject to close scrutiny. For example, according to statistics from the U.S. Department of Education, the number of professors with tenure has remained constant at 52 percent since 1975. This seems good and indicates stable employment, yet closer inspection reveals that the number of professors who were not on the tenure track increased from 19 percent in 1975 to 27 percent in 1993.

Now that the academic job market has dried up, many more PhDs are finding positions in business and industry, some happily and some not so happily (see Chapter 11 for a new Web site for PhD graduates to discuss their experiences with finding jobs outside of academe). The National Science Foundation reports that in 1995 just over 50 percent of PhD graduates in mathematics, engineering, and science were working outside of four year colleges and universities. This percentage has doubled in the last twenty years. Statistics from the National Research Council show a less striking, but still significant, pattern with history PhDs, who have gone from 27 percent who worked outside of four year colleges and universities in 1979 to 36 percent in 1994.

As with the other careers we have covered, it would be impossible to talk about all of the different employment options available to doctoral or master's degree recipients. This section will provide an overview of some of the more popular degree programs and give some insight as to what people with those degrees do for a living. The subjects to be covered are humanities and social sciences, mathematics, social work, computer science, psychology, and engineering.

Humanities and Social Sciences

Included in the humanities and social sciences are history, English, sociology, anthropology, political science, philosophy, geography, archaeology, and foreign languages. The four most common fields where students earn their PhDs are economics, history, English, and political science. In a recent year, just under 1,000 students received a PhD in economics, while approximately 600 received a PhD in political science.

Traditionally, students who have gotten their PhDs in the humanities and social sciences have wanted to teach. The academic job market is quite difficult for these students now. As just one example, at the 1997 American Historical Association's annual meeting job fair, there were 220 positions, and 777 people applied for them.

Mark graduated with a PhD in history from an excellent university. Three months after his graduation, he was working as an office temp doing clerical work as he tried to find a tenure-track position. He was not optimistic about his chances, but he wasn't sure what else he wanted to do.

Although it may be challenging to find jobs in other areas, there are possibilities. If you have a degree in one of the social sciences, you may be able to find a job with a consulting firm, a government agency, a marketing company, a social services organization, or a business. What you will have to offer are your quantitative, communication, and research skills you gained while in graduate school. You could also choose to work for a university as an administrator rather than an academic. This type of job may allow you to teach a class occasionally. The downside of this occupation is that those who are teaching full-time may look down upon you and probably won't treat you as a colleague. The following two paragraphs give you some ideas of some specific jobs you might be able to get if you have a PhD.

History PhDs are sought after to work for nonprofit organizations such as libraries, museums, historical societies, and preservation groups. You could be an editor for a historical papers project. Philosophy PhDs learn strong analytical reasoning and critical thinking skills, which are quite useful in government and business positions. A PhD in archaeology is usually a requirement for a museum curator.

Your PhD in political science qualifies you to conduct public opinion polls for major news organizations and private polling companies. Entering politics, as a campaign manager or political consultant, or working on Capitol Hill or in the executive or judicial branches are possibilities. Corporations that want to open offices abroad hire political science PhDs to perform risk analyses.

The above paragraphs cover PhD graduates, but if you're getting a master's degree, you need to know about some specific jobs that you can get. Having a master's degree can help you to be hired to teach at a community college or private or public high school, although if the PhD market stays as weak as it has been, you may find that you are competing with PhD candidates for some of these teaching positions.

Some master's degree candidates are highly sought after, including those with degrees in urban planning and sociology. Those with master's degrees in English and history can market their skills quite successfully to a variety of businesses, such as publishing companies, and nonprofit organizations, such as museums. If you have a master's degree in anthropology, you will be well trained in quantitative and qualitative research, so you could be hired to do research for businesses, government agencies, and nonprofit organizations.

Government agencies, banks, and accounting firms all hire people with MAs in economics. Your master's degree in geography might be useful to environmental organizations; transportation and planning agencies; and consulting, marketing, and communications firms. If you have a master's degree in political science, public policy, or international affairs, you can use your skills at analyzing policy working for the government, corporations, or consulting firms.

If you have a master's degree in archaeology, you could work in the area of cultural resource management. You might be hired by the federal government (agencies such as the National Park Service or the United States Forest Service), a consulting firm, an oil company, an environmental organization, or a state historic preservation agency. As part of your job, you might help find historic sites, excavate them, and manage them.

Mathematics

You might wonder what you can do with a master's or doctoral degree in mathematics if you don't plan or aren't able to teach at the secondary or post-secondary level. It's wise to be concerned about the academic market, since only 62 employers interviewed at the 1997 American Mathematical Society's job fair, and there were 375 candidates. In 1996, about 9 percent of that year's PhD recipients were unemployed in September. Almost 15 percent of the 1995 PhD recipients found themselves in that situation in September 1995.

There are some jobs outside of academia, though. Mathematicians are hired by the defense industry, investment companies, banks, and insurance companies because of their good analytical and computational skills.

Social Work

The most common social work degree that you will earn is the MSW (Master's of Social Work). It is highly unusual to get a PhD in this field unless you know that you want to enter academia. Because there aren't many social work programs that offer PhDs, the job market for PhDs is predicted to be good in the coming years.

As a social worker, you will work with clients who are having a variety of problems, including trouble with their family, drugs or alcohol, or substandard housing. You may assist individual clients in resolving these problems, or you may work on more of a systemwide basis where you will set policy or be engaged in planning. You may choose to specialize and work primarily with the elderly, children and their families, or the mentally or physically ill.

The most common organizations that hire social workers are government agencies (often state or local social services agencies), nonprofit organizations, or hospitals. You can also be self-employed and provide counseling on your own.

Computer Science

Many people who get a master's degree in computer science do so to gain more practical skills in that field that will allow them to advance within the industry. A PhD can also provide added mobility, but with the high demand for people who are computer literate, a PhD is not necessary. Like social work, this is a field where unless you are certain you want to teach at a university level, you may not want to get a PhD.

Psychology

If you choose to get an advanced degree in psychology, you will choose whether to be a clinical psychologist or a counseling psychologist. More people pick clinical psychology. As a clinical psychologist, you may be involved in research and trying to determine what causes emotional or mental disorders, or you may provide therapy. If you are a counseling psychologist, you will counsel individuals, families, or groups. You may work for a hospital or clinic, have your own practice, or work in a group practice. Some psychologists choose to specialize in areas like careers, substance abuse, or family issues.

If you have a psychology degree, there are many employment opportunities outside of the academy. In addition to the areas mentioned above, you could be hired by a secondary school or a university to provide counseling or by a company to do personnel testing or market research. Organizations that conduct opinion polls hire social psychologists to work on their staffs. Corporations hire psychologists to work in their human resources departments. Cognitive psychologists might be hired by corporations to help make their products appealing to consumers.

Engineering

As with computer science, some people will get a master's degree in engineering simply to learn more about the field and to improve their chances of being promoted more quickly. Since there are a large number of engineers in this country, having a PhD can be an additional credential that will give you more mobility even if you remain in the industrial sector. In addition to the commonly known fields of engineering such as chemical, civil, electrical, and mechanical, there are other specialties, including aerospace, biomedical, environmental, nuclear, petroleum, and materials.

Conclusion

The next chapter on resources will direct you to places where you can learn even more detailed information about specific jobs held by people who have earned your proposed degree. The importance of having a good understanding of the reality of the job market before you enter into a graduate or professional degree program cannot be overstated. You owe it to yourself to be as informed as possible about what you can expect from your investment after you graduate.

chapter 11

Resources

Once you have read this book, you will find that you are quite knowledgeable about whatever graduate or professional degree you want to pursue. Yet, there is still much more detailed information available to you from a wide variety of sources. You'll be doing yourself a favor to read as much as possible so you can be an informed consumer. This chapter will give you information about the following areas:

- General information
- Standardized tests
- Test preparation
- Common applications
- Financial aid
- Credit reporting agencies
- Professional associations
- Graduate school

General Information

A student at MIT started a Web site that includes links to the home pages of many universities in the United States and abroad. What started as a relatively minor project has now mushroomed into a site that has links to over 3,000 university home pages, which can be found using an alphabetical or geographical index. The site is **http://www.mit.edu:8001/people/cdemello/univ.html.**

If you're looking for a discussion group on graduate school, you can check out **http://www.petersons.com/ugrad/discuss/wwwboard.html**, or **http://www.review.com/index.shtml**.

Standardized Tests

The agencies that administer the standardized tests are your key resource for specific information about each of the standardized tests. They can tell you when the tests are scheduled, how you can register for them, how much they cost, and how to prepare for them. The standard packet of information sent out on your initial request contains all of this information and also has sample test questions. Most of the agencies also sell test preparation materials, which may include old copies of past tests that have been administered.

Each of the agencies' Web sites give you the same information you can get in written format, and they offer links to other sites that might be of interest to you, including links to graduate and professional schools' Web pages.

Graduate Management Admission Test (GMAT)

GMAT
Educational Testing Service
P.O. Box 6103
Princeton, NJ 08541-6103
Phone: (609) 771-7330
Fax: (609) 883-4349
gmat@ets.org
http://www.gmat.org

Law School Admission Test (LSAT)

Law Services
Box 2400
661 Penn Street
Newtown, PA 18940-0977
Phone: (215) 968-1314
Fax: (215) 968-1169
http://www.lsac.org

Law Services publishes *The Official Guide to U.S. Law Schools* ($17.00), which contains a description of each of the accredited law schools in the United States and also contains general information about law schools and the admissions process. It also publishes *So You Want to Be a Lawyer: A Practical Guide* ($10.00).

Graduate Record Examination (GRE)

Graduate Record Examinations
Educational Testing Service
P.O. Box 6000
Princeton, NJ 08541-6000
Phone: (609) 771-7670
Fax: (609) 771-7906
(800) 537-3160 (for publications)
gre-info@ets.org
http://www.ets.org

Medical College Admission Test (MCAT)

For registration information for the MCAT, you should contact the MCAT program office.

MCAT Program Office
P.O. Box 4056
Iowa City, IA 52243
Phone: (319) 337-1357

For general information regarding the MCAT and to get test preparation materials, you should contact the Association of American Medical Colleges (AAMC). AAMC also publishes *Medical School Admission Requirements*, an annual publication which provides information about the admissions process and about each of the medical schools in theUnited States.

AAMC
Membership and Publication Orders
2450 N Street, NW
Washington, DC 20037
Phone: (202) 828-0416
mcat@aamc.org

Test Preparation

The two biggest and best-known test preparation companies are Kaplan and The Princeton Review. Both offer test preparation courses and test preparation books that you can purchase to study on your own. The courses cost around $1,000. The books cost around $25–$30. Reread Chapter 4 if you need help deciding whether to take a test preparation course or to prepare on your own.

Kaplan Educational Centers
888 7th Avenue
New York, NY 10106
Phone: (800) KAP-TEST
http://www.kaplan.com

The Princeton Review
2315 Broadway
New York, NY 10024
Phone: (800) REVIEW-6
http://www.review.com

Common Applications

Chapter 5 mentioned that there are two companies that sell computer products that contain applications for more than one school. These are the products where you just have to enter common information once and then they fill it into the right spots on each application. Contact information for these two companies is listed below.

Membership Collaborative Services, Inc. (MCS)
740 S. Chester Road, Suite F
Swarthmore, PA 19081
Phone: (800) 516-2227
mcs@multi-app.com
http://www.multi-app.com

MCS offers Law Multi-App and Business Multi-App, which are disks that contain applications for 63 law schools and 55 business schools. The cost is $65.00 for either the business school disk or the law school disk. You can download the information from MCS's Web site, but to print the applications, you have to have the source code, which costs $59.00.

Law Services
Box 2400
Newtown, PA 18940-0977
Phone: (215) 968-1001
http://www.lsac.org

Law Services offers a CD-ROM that contains the applications for all of the ABA-approved law schools. The CD-ROM also has the complete contents of *The Official Guide to Law Schools,* Law Services' publication that has information on all of the law schools.

Medical School Admissions

As mentioned in Chapter 5 on the admissions process, almost all medical schools participate in one of the following three common application systems. Check with your medical schools to find out which system(s) you need to use. Obtaining all of these applications is free. The cost occurs when you submit the applications.

AMCAS
Section for Student Services
2501 M Street, NW, Lobby-26
Washington, DC 20037-1300
amcas@aamc.org
http://www.aamc.org

University of Texas System Medical and Dental Application Center (UTSMDAC)
702 Colorado, Suite 620
Austin, TX 78701
crutledge@utsystem.edu

Ontario Medical School Application Service (OMSAS)
P.O. Box 1328
650 Woodlawn Road West
Guelph, Ontario, Canada N1H 7P4
omsas@netserv.ouac.on.ca

Financial Aid

As you read in Chapter 8 on financial aid, there are many sources of financial aid available to you. By using the resources in the following list, you can become an expert on financial aid and clearly understand what options are available to you to pay for your graduate or professional school education. You will also find great sources of information on how you can find free money in the form of scholarships, grants, and fellowships.

General Financial Aid Information

http://www.finaid.org or http://www.finaid.com

This incredible Web site is maintained by the National Association of Financial Aid Administrators (NASFAA) and can be found using either of the above two addresses. It is a very thorough and objective guide to financial aid and has links to almost every other Web page that has any information about financial aid. This is an excellent starting point for financial aid questions of all types.

Another good source of general financial aid information is the Department of Education Student Guide, which can be found at **http://www.ed.gov/prog_info/SFA/Student Guide/**.

A Web site that lists links to lots of other financial aid Web sites, where you can find out about loans and scholarships is **http://www.collegiate.net/infoa4.html**.

Law Services
Box 2400
661 Penn Street
Newtown, PA 18940-0977
Phone: (215) 968-1314
http://www.lsac.org

Law Services publishes *Financial Aid for Law School: A Preliminary Guide* (free).

Loans

There are many lenders who you can use to get federal loans. If you had federal loans as an undergraduate, you may wish to use the same lender for graduate or professional school. This is a good choice if you don't plan to borrow any private loans, since that way you will only have to deal with one lender during repayment. If you plan to borrow private loans and federal loans during graduate or professional school, you may want to find a lender who offers both federal and private loans. Then you will be able to use only one lender during your graduate work. Some of the bigger lenders for graduate and professional school are: Nellie Mae, The Access Group, Sallie Mae, Citibank, and TERI (The Education Resources Institute).

Nellie Mae
50 Braintree Hill Park, Suite 300
Braintree, MA 02184
Phone: (800) 988-4846 or (800) 634-9308
info@nelliemae.org
http://www.nelliemae.org

Nellie Mae is the largest nonprofit lender in the United States. It offers the EXCEL loans to graduate, law, business, and medical students.

The Access Group
Box 7430
Wilmington, DE 19803
Phone: (800) 282-1550
general@accessgrp.org
http://www.accessgrp.org

The Access Group offers federal and private loans for graduate school, law school, business school, and medical school. Their Web page includes Access Advisor, a free comprehensive debt management program. They also provide Need Access, an electronic need analysis application service for graduate and professional schools.

Citibank Student Loans
P.O. Box 22948
Rochester, NY 14692
Phone: (800) 967-8677
https://studentloan.citibank.com/slc/

Citibank offers federal and private loans for graduate, and professional students. The Web site is quite informative.

Sallie Mae offers loans for law students (Law Loans), medical students (MedLoans), and MBA Students (MBA Loans). They have a very comprehensive Web site that lists the terms and conditions of each loan and gives you lots of other financial aid information. That address is **http://www.salliemae.com/aud/cao/**. You can also call 800-984-0190 for Law Loans, 800-858-5050 for MedLoans, and 888-440-4622(4MBA) for MBA Loans.

The Education Resources Institute (TERI)
330 Stuart Street, Suite 500
Boston, MA 02116-5237
Phone: (800) 255-8374
custserv@teri.org
http://www.teri.org

TERI offers federal loans PEP (Professional Education Program) loans for graduate and professional students. TERI publishes a useful resource, *Graduating Into Debt: The Burdens of Borrowing for Graduate & Professional Students.*

The Federal government can provide information on Federal loan programs. You can also complete the Free Application for Federal Student Aid on the Web, using **http://www.fafsa.ed.gov**.

Stafford Loan Program
The Federal Student Aid Information Center
P.O. Box 84
Washington, DC 20044
Phone: (800) 433-3243 ((800) 4-FED-AID)
http://www.ed.gov/offices/OPE/express.html

Scholarships and Grants

When you're looking for scholarships, Web sites are a good place to start because they are free and easy to access. If you are interested in some of the books that are listed below, you may want to check with your university library or public library to see if they have them so that you don't have to purchase them.

A terrific source of information for scholarships is called Fast Web. Using this service, you can search for scholarships that match your background and area of interest. The Web site is **http://www.studentservices.com/fastweb/.**

The Web site located at **http://www.studentservices.com** provides information on over 180,000 scholarships, grants, and loans available from the private sector.

The Foundation Center is an independent, nonprofit organization that serves as an information clearinghouse regarding foundations and grants. The Center publishes *Foundation Grants to Individuals*, which has entries for 3,200 foundations that give grants to individuals. The book contains six indexes to help you use it most effectively. The 1997 edition costs $65.00 and can be ordered from **http://fdncenter.org**.

Another, less comprehensive, source of information on grants from foundations is *Foundation Grants for Individuals.* It is free and is available from:

National Commission for Cooperative Education
360 Huntington Ave.
Suite 384CP
Boston, MA 02115

The Jacob K. Javits Foundation offers fellowships in the arts, humanities, and social sciences. Call (202) 260-3574 for more information.

The Andrew W. Mellon Foundation provides fellowships for PhD students who are in their first year of study and who plan to pursue teaching. For more information, you can check the Web site at **www.woodrow.org/mellon** or call (609) 452-7007.

The National Science Foundation provides fellowships for graduate students in the social sciences (anthropology, sociology, economics) as well as those in the sciences. They have a free publication called *A Selected List of Fellowship Opportunities and Aids to Advanced Education for U.S. Citizens and Foreign Nationals.* For more information, you can call (423) 241-4300 or write to:

Publications Office
4201 Wilson Blvd.
Arlington, VA 22230

If you are a minority who plans to pursue engineering or the sciences, you may want to investigate GEM Fellowships. Information about them is available by writing:

1118 N. Eddy Street
South Bend, IN 46617
or calling (219) 631-7771

Chapter 8 mentioned that the National Health Service Corps has a scholarship program for medical students who are willing to work in rural areas after graduation from medical school. Information about the program can be obtained by writing:

National Health Service Corps
2070 Chain Bridge Road
Vienna, VA 22182
or calling (800) 221-9393

You may find the following books helpful in your search for scholarships, grants, or fellowships. You would be well advised to try to find them in a library rather than purchase them.

Bauer, David G., *The Complete Grants Sourcebook for Higher Education,* 3rd ed. Oryx Press, 1995.

The Black Collegian's Guide to Graduate and Professional Fellowships for Minority Students. 5th ed. New Orleans, LA: The Black Collegian, 1994.

Cassidy, Daniel. *The Graduate Scholarship Book: The Complete Guide to Scholarships, Fellowships, Grants, and Loans for Graduate and Professional Study.* 2nd ed. National Scholarship Reference Service, Prentice-Hall, 1990.

Directory of Biomedical and Health Care Grants, 1995. 9th ed. Oryx Press, 1995.

Directory of Grants in the Humanities: 1995–96. 9th ed. Oryx Press 1995.

Gale Research Inc. *Scholarships, Fellowships, and Loans 1996.* Volume 11, no. 96. Gale Research Inc.: Detroit, 1995.

Maloney, Wendy A. *Grants, Fellowships, and Prizes of Interest to Historians: 1994–1995.* Washington, DC: American Historical Association, 1994.

National Endowment for the Arts. *Literature: Application Guidelines Fiscal Year 1995.* Washington DC: National Endowment for the Arts, 1995.

Schlacther, Gail Ann, and R. David Weber. *Financial Aid for the Disabled and their Families: 1994–1996.* San Carlos, CA: Reference Service Press, 1994.

Williams, Lisa (ed.). *The Grants Register 1995–1997.* New York: St. Martin's Press, 1994.

Unfortunately, along with all of the legitimate scholarships that are offered, there are some scholarship scams operating as well. You can check out the latest scholarship scams on the Web site **http://www.finaid.org/finaid/scams.html**.

Credit Reporting Agencies

There are four national credit reporting agencies. Since different companies can report their findings to different credit agencies, it's a good idea to check with all four to find out if there are negative reports with any of them. If you have been denied credit within the last 60 days, the agencies will give you a report for free. Otherwise, they may charge a nominal fee.

TRW Consumer Assistance Center
P.O. Box 2350
Chatsworth, CA 91313-2350
Phone: (800) 682-7654

CBI/Equifax
P.O. Box 105873
Atlanta, GA 30348
Phone: (800) 685-1111

Trans Union Corporation
P.O. Box 390
Springfield, PA 19064-0390
Phone: (215) 690-6100

CSC Credit Services
P.O. Box 674402
Houston, TX 77267-4402
Phone: (800) 759-5979

Professional Associations

Professional associations can often provide you with additional information regarding career opportunities in your chosen field. Different associations can provide varying amounts of information, so be sure to ask for anything they can give you that would be helpful. There will be a fee charged for most of the publications listed here, so you may want to call first and find out more information about a publication to determine whether it is worth your investment.

Many associations sponsor professional conferences that you may be able to attend, even if you are just considering attending graduate school in that area. Associations may also have information about grants, fellowships, or scholarships that are unique to their discipline.

Law

American Bar Association (ABA)
Section of Legal Education and Admissions to the Bar
750 N. Lake Shore Drive
Chicago, IL 60611
http://www.abanet.org/legaled

The ABA publishes numerous books that might be helpful to someone who is considering law school. *ABA Approved Law Schools: Statistical*

Information on American Bar Association Approved Schools lists comparative information about each of the law schools in the country. The ABA also publishes a series of books on *Careers in ...* (Sports Law, Natural Resources and Environmental Law, Labor Law, International Law, Entertainment Law, Admiralty and Marine Law, and Civil Litigation).

National Association for Law Placement (NALP)
1666 Connecticut Avenue, NW
Washington, DC 20009-1039
Phone: (202) 667-1666
http://www.nalp.org

NALP publishes materials that help law students make informed career choices. It also maintains statistics on the employment experiences of recent law school graduates.

Business

American Management Association
135 W. 50th Street
New York, NY 10020-1201

Association of MBA Executives
207 Commerce Street
East Haven, CT 06512

The Graduate Management Admission Council publishes a free brochure, *MBA Q & A*, which provides some information about MBA careers and other questions people have about MBA programs. You can request a copy at *http://www.gmat.org*, where you can also get answers to questions about MBA careers.

Medicine

American Medical Student Association (AMSA)
1902 Association Drive
Reston, VA 20191
Phone: (800) 767-2266
Fax: (703) 620-5873
amsa@www.amsa.org
http://www.amsa.org

AMSA has many useful publications and resources for current and prospective medical students. A few of the more helpful publications are *Choosing a Career*, available for $6.75; *AMSA's Student Guide to the Appraisal and Selection of House Staff Training Programs*, available for $8.00, which assists you in applying for and selecting a residency program; and *Survival Manual: A Guide to the Clinical Years*, available for $13.00.

Health (MPH or MHA)

Association of University Programs in Health Administration
1911 N. Fort Myer Drive, Suite 503
Arlington, VA 22209
(703) 524-5500

This association can provide information about graduate academic programs. The Accrediting Commission on Education for Health Services Administration is at the same address and can provide a list of accredited graduate programs in health services administration.

Biology

American Institute of Biological Sciences
730 11th Street NW
Washington, DC 20001-4521
Phone: (202) 628-1509

This institute publishes *Careers in Biology III*, which outlines careers in the field. It also contains an extensive list of professional associations in biological sciences subdisciplines.

Chemistry

American Chemical Society (ACS)
1155 Sixteenth Street NW
Washington, DC 20036
Phone: (202) 872-4414

The ACS publishes the *ACS Directory of Graduate Research,* which lists chemistry departments in the United States and Canada. This directory includes information about professors and programs. The ACS also publishes *Planning for Graduate Work in Chemistry, and Current Trends in Chemical Technology, Business, and Employment,* which assesses the state of chemistry business and employment.

Physics

American Institute of Physics
American Center for Physics
1 Physics Ellipse
College Park, MD 20740
Phone: (301) 209-3007

This institute publishes *Graduate Programs in Physics, Astronomy, and Related Fields,* which gives information about programs, departments, and faculty.

Computer Science

Computing Research Association
1875 Connecticut Avenue NW, Suite 718
Washington, DC 20009
Phone: (202) 234-2111

This association publishes the *Graduate School Information Kit* and the *Forsythe List,* which is a complete list of all PhD programs in computer science and computer engineering. You can also ask for the Taulbee Survey which includes information on PhD programs and faculty in computer science and computer engineering.

Engineering

The American Society for Engineering Education (ASEE)
1818 N Street NW, Suite 600
Washington, DC 20036-2479
Phone: (202) 331-3500
Fax: (202) 265-8504
http://www.asee.org

ASEE publishes the annual *Directory of Graduate Engineering Statistics,* which provides extensive statistical information on graduate engineering departments. It compares enrollments, degrees awarded, faculty summaries, and student appointments with the average monthly stipends. The book is not cheap ($100), so if you're interested, you may want to find a copy you can borrow.

Psychology

American Psychological Association (APA)
750 First Street NE
Washington, DC 20002-4242
Phone: (202) 336-5500
http://www.apa.org

The APA publishes *Graduate Study in Psychology,* a directory of over 500 graduate programs in counseling and psychology. It is 592 pages and costs $19.95. Another admissions resource is *Getting In: A Step by Step Plan for Gaining Admission to Graduate School in Psychology.* It is 221 pages and costs $14.95. Since graduate programs in psychology are some of the most competitive to get into, this resource may well be a valuable investment, although it was published in 1993. If you are interested in what career you might pursue in psychology, you can order the free 37-page booklet, *Psychology: Scientific Problem Solvers —Careers for the 21st Century.* The booklet contains career and salary information and career profiles of people working in psychology.

Sociology

American Sociological Association
1722 N Street NW
Washington, DC 20036-2981
Phone: (202) 833-3410

English and Other Languages

Modern Language Association (MLA)
10 Astor Place
New York, NY 10003
Phone: (212) 475-9500
http://www.mla.org

The MLA's Web site contains information on books and journals, its annual convention, and its job service. The MLA publishes *The MLA Guide to the Job Search,* which gives advice to PhDs on getting hired by colleges and universities and also talks about how PhDs in the humanities can find jobs outside of higher education.

Anthropology

American Anthropological Association (AAA)
4350 N. Fairfax Drive, Suite 640
Arlington, VA 22203
Phone: (703) 528-1902
http://www.ameranthassn.org

The AAA's Web site contains the text of a brochure, *Careers in Anthropology: Education for the 21st Century* that discusses why you might want to study anthropology and what you can do with a degree in that field.

Geography

Association of American Geographers
1710 16th Street NW
Washington, DC 20009-3198
Phone: (202) 234-1450

This association publishes *A Guide to Programs of Geography in the U.S. and Canada,* which lists schools that have programs in geography. It also publishes *Geography: Today's Career for Tomorrow,* which is available free of charge, and *Careers in Geography,* available for $3.00.

History

American Historical Association (AHA)
400 A Street SE
Washington, DC 20003
Phone: (202) 544-2422
http://www.gmu.edu

The AHA publishes a guide to graduate programs in history.

Political Science

American Political Science Association (APSA)
1527 New Hampshire Avenue NW
Washington, DC 20036
Phone: (202) 483-2512
http://www.apsanet.org

APSA publishes *Careers and the Study of Political Science: A Guide for Undergraduates.* It costs $4.50. APSA's Web site also has a section on grants and fellowships.

Public Administration

National Association of Schools of Public Affairs and Administration
1120 G Street NW, Suite 730
Washington, DC 20005
Phone: (202) 628-8965

This association publishes *Programs in Public Affairs and Administration.* It is published every other year and contains information on various programs, how they are taught, and what kinds of students they attract.

Education

American Association of Colleges for Teacher Education
One Dupont Circle NW, Suite 610
Washington, DC 20036-2412
Phone: (202) 293-2450

American Federation of School Administrators
1729 21st Street NW
Washington, DC 20009
Phone: (202) 986-4209

American Association of School Administrators
1801 N. Moore Street
Arlington, VA 22209
Phone: (703) 528-0700

Social Work

Council on Social Work Education
1600 Duke Street
Alexandria, VA 22314-3421
Phone: (703) 683-8080

Graduate School

The Council of Graduate Schools (CGS) is a consortium of member schools that provides a variety of services. Of particular interest to a prospective graduate student is CGS's Web site, which has links to the Web sites for all of its member schools. CGS also publishes two books that might be of help. One is *Graduate School and You: A Guide for Prospective Graduate Students.* It is 136 pages, was published in 1995, and costs $5.00. CGS also publishes *The Essential Guide to Graduate Admissions,* which costs $10.00.

Council of Graduate Schools (CGS)
One Dupont Circle, NW, Suite 430
Washington, DC 20036-1173
Phone: (202) 223-3791
Fax: (202) 331-7157
http://www.cgsnet.org

If you want to know how to get the most out of graduate school, there are two Web sites to check out. One is How to Succeed in Graduate School and can be found at **www.erg.sri.com/people/marie/papers/advice-summary.html.** The other is Graduate School Survival Guide and can be found at **http://smi.stanford.edu/people/pratt/smi/advice.html.** Both have great suggestions on the best ways to approach graduate school.

Graduate Student Resources on the Web, **http://www-personal.umich.edu/~danhorn/graduate.html,** is a site that directs you to lots of other sites having to do with graduate school.

Doctoral Recipients

There are a few general resources that are available to people who have received their PhDs (or who might be thinking about getting a PhD) that are related to careers. One is *On the Market: Surviving the Academic Job Search* by Christina Boufis and Victoria C. Olsen (Riverside Books). This book is a compilation of 40 essays from those who have gotten their PhDs. It includes advice on the application process, job interviews, and alternative careers.

Another resource is a Web site that was started by four PhD graduates in literature who went to work in business after they received their PhDs. They started the Web site to share their job search experiences and to start a conversation with others who are in or have been in the same situation. The Web site is **http://members.aol.com/phdswork/welcome.html**.

A third initiative is called Preparing Future Faculty and is a joint effort of the Association of American Colleges and Universities and the Council of Graduate Schools. One hundred and eight colleges and universities participate in the project, which is designed to give graduate students a better idea of what they can expect in the academic profession. More information about this project can be found at **http://www.preparing-faculty.org/**. The Web site also contains a job service.

Conclusion

As you can see from this chapter, there is a wealth of information available to you on all aspects of graduate and professional school. Don't forget, of course, that the schools themselves have many materials you can request that will give you useful information about that school. This information includes admissions literature, the catalog of courses, and financial aid information, to name the most obvious. Surfing the Web is also a good way to uncover additional information that you may find helpful.

Index

A

B

C

D

E

F

G

I

J

K

L

M

N

O

P

R

S

T

U

V

W

REAL LIFE GUIDES—Spring 1998

Real Life Guide to Life After College, Second Edition
ISBN 1-890586-06-4

The #1 Guide for a successful transition from college to real life. Graduates receive hard hitting information and advice from the experts. Real Life insight into job hunting, interviewing skills, personal finance, Internet resources and relocation. (300 pages)

Suggested Retail $16.95

Real Life Guide to Starting Your Career ISBN 1-890586-02-1

Plan and execute your job search like an experienced professional even though you aren't one. Written specifically for recent graduates, this book will give you the critical information you need to prepare your resume, interview, negotiate your salary, and thrive once you are on board. (300 pages)

Suggested Retail. $16.95

Real Life Guide to Graduate and Professional School
ISBN 1-890586-05-6

Whether you are considering graduate or professional school, or you are already knee deep in research projects, this book will be your best friend. Identify the best strategy for achieving your academic pursuits and apply them to the real world. (350 pages)

Suggested Retail $27.95

Real Life Guide to Internet Resources for Graduates
ISBN 1-890586-04-8

Navigate your way directly to the best resources for graduates. Hand picked by our Internet gurus specifically for recent college graduates, these sites are the best the Internet has to offer you. The PowerTool CD takes directly to the web resources you need. (220 pages)

Suggested Retail $16.95

Each Real Life Guide includes a PowerTool CD

- View the entire contents of the book through your web browser
- Get on the Internet with MindSpring
- Save time and energy with WebPrinter
- Real Life Resource list points you straight to the Internet's best
- Other valuable software pertinent to the book topic

About the PowerTool CD-ROM

The CD-ROM included with your copy of your *Real Life Guide to Graduate and Professional School* contains valuable software, files, links, and an HTML Version of the book. Read on for more information about the contents of the CD-ROM and how to use it.

Navigating the CD-ROM

Windows users can navigate through the CD-ROM contents via the Windows 3.1x File Manager or Windows 95/NT Windows Explorer. Macintosh users need to simply double click on the CD-ROM and any resulting folders they wish to view.

Even though there are no programs for any other operating system on this CD-ROM, other systems can access the HTML files through the operating system interface to the CD-ROM.

Programs

This CD-ROM contains useful software and resources to supplement the book. Your Real Life Guide PowerTool CD-ROM includes the following:

MindSpring PipeLine+ 2.6 (http://www.mindspring.com)

The MindSpring software includes various helper applications in addition to the connectivity software. These helper applications include Eudora, Free Agent, Chat, WS-FTP, Telnet, Talk, Lview Pro, WinCode, Finger, Ping, Internet Explorer 3, and WinZip. Getting online has never been easier than with MindSpring! To install the MindSpring PipeLine+ software, you will simply need to launch the following installers:

Windows: "d:\programs\msprinst\setup.exe" (where d: is the drive letter of your CD-ROM drive)
Macintosh: Inside the "MindSpring" folder, double click on "Mindspring Install.1" When prompted to enter the "Registration Key" please enter "PIPE-0309" without the quotation marks. Your registration will then continue.

WebPrinter 2.0 (http://www.ffg.com)

This Windows 3.1x and Windows95 program will instantly turn your valuable Internet, CD-ROM and Windows data into attractive booklets. With only two clicks, sports stats, custom travel itineraries, financial "how-to" guides, product literature, maps and even photos are transformed into convenient, double-sided booklets.

Resources

This folder on the CD-ROM contains files that are supplemental to the contents of the book. Each of these files can be accessed by clicking the links at the top of the page. The files are the following:

Major City Classified Links

This pages contains links to online classifieds for 80 of the United States and Canada's major cities.

Real Life Resources for Graduate & Professional School

Links to many of the Net's best resources for Graduate & Professional School candidates. Not only will you find a link to the site's listed, but you will also find a brief description on each to help you gage your time.

Limits of Liability & Disclaimer of Warranty

The authors and publisher of this book have made their best effort in preparing this CD-ROM and any programs it contains. The authors and publisher make no warranty of any kind expressed or implied, with regard to these programs or the documentation contained in this book.

The authors and publisher shall not be liable in the event of incidental or consequential damages in connection with, or arising out of, the furnishing, performance, or use of the programs, associated instructions, and/or claims of productivity gains. Please view any addition documentation with any of the files on this CD-ROM for more information.